SUCCESSFUL MEETINGS

How to Plan, Prepare, and Execute Top-Notch Business Meetings

Shri Henkel

SUCCESSFUL MEETINGS: HOW TO PLAN, PREPARE, AND EXECUTE TOP-NOTCH BUSINESS MEETINGS

Copyright © 2007 by Atlantic Publishing Group, Inc.
1210 SW 23rd Place • Ocala, Florida 34474 • 800-814-1132 • 352-622-5836–Fax
Web site: www.atlantic-pub.com • E-mail: sales@atlantic-pub.com
SAN Number: 268-1250

ISBN-13: 978-0-910627-91-7   ISBN-10: 0-910627-91-6

Library of Congress Cataloging-in-Publication Data

Henkel, Shri L., 1965-
  Successful meetings : how to plan, prepare, and execute top-notch business meetings / by Shri L. Henkel.
      p. cm.
  Includes bibliographical references and index.
  ISBN-13: 978-0-910627-91-7 (alk. paper)
  ISBN-10: 0-910627-91-6 (alk. paper)
  1. Business meetings. 2. Business meetings--Planning. I. Title.

  HF5734.5.H46 2007
  658.4'56--dc22
                          2006035300

EDITOR: Marie Lujanac, mlujanac817@yahoo.com
PROOFREADER: Angela C. Adams, angela.c.adams@hotmail.com
ART DIRECTION: Meg Buchner • megadesn@mchsi.com

Printed in the United States

CONTENTS

CHAPTER 3 THE WHO, WHAT, AND WHEN OF YOUR MEETING 45

CHAPTER 7   EFFECTIVE WAYS TO START YOUR MEETING   123

CHAPTER 8   CONDUCT EFFECTIVE MEETINGS 137

CHAPTER 9   ELEMENTS OF AN EFFECTIVE MEETING   161

DEDICATION

This book is dedicated to all managers and other employees or members who are facing their first meeting. It is also dedicated to the meeting leaders who want to make a difference in the meetings they conduct.

I hope the information within these pages help you conduct effective and successful meetings that will enlighten and help your employees or group members.

Finally, this book is dedicated to my grandfather, John Henkel, who showed me the value of working hard for my employers and the importance of giving superior customer service to bring the customers back. And to my grandmother, Hannah Gum, who works hard and showed me what a woman can accomplish. I wouldn't have accomplished as much without their great examples.

We recently lost our beloved pet "Bear," who was not only our best and dearest friend but also the "Vice President of Sunshine" here at Atlantic Publishing. He did not receive a salary but worked tirelessly 24 hours a day to please his parents. Bear was a rescue dog that turned around and showered myself, my wife Sherri, his grandparents Jean, Bob and Nancy and every person and animal he met (maybe not rabbits) with friendship and love. He made a lot of people smile every day.

We wanted you to know that a portion of the profits of this book will be donated to The Humane Society of the United States. –*Douglas & Sherri Brown*

The human-animal bond is as old as human history. We cherish our animal companions for their unconditional affection and acceptance. We feel a thrill when we glimpse wild creatures in their natural habitat or in our own backyard.

Unfortunately, the human-animal bond has at times been weakened. Humans have exploited some animal species to the point of extinction.

The Humane Society of the United States makes a difference in the lives of animals here at home and worldwide. The HSUS is dedicated to creating a world where our relationship with animals is guided by compassion. We seek a truly humane society in which animals are respected for their intrinsic value, and where the human-animal bond is strong.

Want to help animals? We have plenty of suggestions. Adopt a pet from a local shelter, join The Humane Society and be a part of our work to help companion animals and wildlife. You will be funding our educational, legislative, investigative and outreach projects in the U.S. and across the globe.

Or perhaps you'd like to make a memorial donation in honor of a pet, friend or relative? You can through our Kindred Spirits program. And if you'd like to contribute in a more structured way, our Planned Giving Office has suggestions about estate planning, annuities, and even gifts of stock that avoid capital gains taxes.

Maybe you have land that you would like to preserve as a lasting habitat for wildlife. Our Wildlife Land Trust can help you. Perhaps the land you want to share is a backyard—that's enough. Our Urban Wildlife Sanctuary Program will show you how to create a habitat for your wild neighbors.

So you see, it's easy to help animals. And The HSUS is here to help.

THE HUMANE SOCIETY OF THE UNITED STATES®

2100 L Street NW • Washington, DC 20037 • 202-452-1100
www.hsus.org

FOREWORD

The minute someone says to me, "We need to have a meeting," I tend to hear a high-pitched whine of resistance (sounds sort of like, "Oh, noooooooooooo!), and I start looking for the door rather than my planner. People grow to hate meetings.

Have you ever shown up promptly for a meeting, only to have two or three people straggle in late while the person in charge of the meeting shuffles through a briefcase, looks through notes at the last minute, rearranges chairs and coffee mugs, and wastes time waiting for absolutely every invitee to arrive before convening the meeting? Have you ever been a participant in a team presentation during an hour-long meeting when the presenter ahead of you exceeds his five minutes allotted on the agenda and is only halfway through his presentation at ten minutes and counting? Have you ever listened as one windbag monopolizes 20 minutes of an hour-long meeting with her personal vision on a topic that should only have taken two minutes of the agenda? Have you ever attended a one-hour meeting that wound up being a two- or (you know it!) three-hour meeting? Have you ever shown up at a meeting where there was no agenda so that the topics that needed to be addressed never were covered?

I've worked in the professional world for longer than I care to say and have been to and organized more meetings than I can count. Some were great, the majority needed a lot of improvement, and a few were downright mind-numbingly dull or abysmally disorganized. I've been a member of Toastmasters for more than 14 years, and our worldwide organization insists on members' learning how to begin and end meetings on time and how to plan meetings from start to finish. Effective use of time shows respect for our fellow human beings.

Fortunately, Shri Henkel can show you the way to have successful meetings. Shri's book is one I am proud to have on my library shelf and one that I'll continue to recommend to all business associates as well as my fellow Toastmasters. Read on, and no more whining!

June A. Van Valkenburg
Owner—Visibilities 360, LLC
www.visibilities360.com

Toastmaster Experience
Distinguished Toastmaster – Estrella Toastmasters, Goodyear, Arizona
Toastmasters Experience – President three times, Vice President of Education four times, Vice President of Public Relations two times, Vice President Secretary/Treasurer two times, Vice President of Membership one time. Also worked with District leadership serving as Area Governor for two terms (an Area consists of four to six clubs)
Club Coach Committee Chair for Toastmasters International District Three (which consists of 176 clubs in Arizona)

Business Experience
Aerospace Policies and Procedures - Administrative Support
Magazine Publishing - Art Director and Freelance Graphic Design
Civil Engineering - Administrative Support
Manufacturing – Management
Education - Adjunct Faculty

INTRODUCTION

When you think of business meetings, what comes to mind? Do you see a group of people sitting in a crowded room wasting their time? As the leader, chair, or facilitator of meetings, would you like to change deficient content into efficient accomplishment?

Why do meetings fail? Conflict, disruption, straying from the subject, a negative or threatening vibe, an unprepared speaker, miscommunication, undefined purpose, use of unfamiliar jargon, confusion, broken technical equipment, repetition ("We've heard this a hundred times!"), no spark? This book is written to help you improve the quality of your meetings either as leader or participant. Here you will discover the tools and creative techniques to handle these obstacles.

Thankfully, I have experienced the rare, effective meeting and I have successful meeting leaders and conductors who share their secrets throughout this book. We start with basics to explain what a meeting should be and how to evaluate whether you actually need one. (There must be legitimate reasons for holding meetings. There are so many of them!) We discuss your initial planning, setting your objectives, developing an effective agenda, and settling on the proper way to start meetings to accomplish your goals. Along the way we offer many tips and suggestions to keep your meeting moving briskly.

With a little planning and communication everyone will know beforehand what to expect at the meeting: who will attend, where it will be held, and its purpose and goals. Speakers and presenters need to know what to do before, during, and after the meeting, and the better you know the people in attendance, the better you can shape the agenda to be effective for them.

All facets of business require effective communication, particularly meetings, one of the best opportunities to set a positive tone for communication. We tell you how to strike the right chord, get the feedback, and what to do with that feedback. We share a variety of techniques to encourage participation, a hallmark of a successful meeting.

Have you ever used handouts, posters, or other tools in your meetings? Chapter 12 discusses which tools to use and how to make them more effective, including preparing and displaying information for the greatest impact.

Successful meetings need a definite conclusion, sometimes by reaching a consensus. Other times, you just need to wrap it up, giving the people in attendance a feeling of completion. When your meeting is over, evaluate your performance and the success of the meeting by gathering feedback using checklists and questionnaires. They are included here along with room layouts, meeting terms, and secrets of effective meetings from the pros.

Does your boss appreciate employees who show initiative? This book is written for the meeting conductor, but participants will gain a better understanding of the effort and skills required to run a successful meeting. If you are now merely occupying a seat at numbers of meetings, you will be enabled to offer to set up and conduct meetings, a good way to stand out from the crowd and become valuable to your employer. Now let us turn the page and start learning how to have effective, successful meetings.

1

MEETING BASICS

———

Since many people have never attended an effective, productive meeting, let's examine one. The overall goal is to have the attendees feel they have learned or accomplished something—not always easy, but it can be done. Here are your first steps.

FIRST CONSIDERATION: DO YOU *NEED* A FACE-TO-FACE MEETING?

Is it necessary to meet in one place? Would another means of communication work just as well? Consider your reasons for bringing people together:

- The need to make a major decision and gather input from the people involved.

- The need to provide additional training to employees.

- The need for a quick response from certain people to solve an urgent problem.

- The need to convince a potential client to work with you or your company.

Some of these objectives can be accomplished by a memo, report, phone call, online chats, or a Web cast. Each of these options has various benefits.

Cost

The overriding consideration in how to communicate with a group is comparative costs. The most obvious expenses include possible travel, transportation, or rental of A-V equipment and meeting site, and refreshments. However, the bottom line is most affected by payroll cost, which is larger than most people realize.

When you consider the payroll cost, figure how many people will attend and for how long. For example, the meeting is two hours long for which each attendee will be paid. It is inevitable that they will socialize or linger over refreshments and take extra time getting back to their desks and more time getting refocused on work. The best case scenario would be 2-½ hours away from work per person.

What would that cost for a two-hour meeting with 50 people. We will estimate that each person makes $10 an hour, which is probably low for any meeting.

50 people at $10 per hour = $500 for each hour of the meeting

Two-hour meeting at $500 per hour = $1,000 in payroll for meeting

A half hour for people to get to work = $250 in additional payroll for wasted time

The meeting cost $1,250 in payroll expenses for its duration, not counting the hours spent preparing the meeting materials and agenda. All these expenses must be included when you are deciding whether a meeting is the best choice for each situation.

Restrictions

Sometimes there is no time for a meeting. Do you have

- Time to prepare for an effective meeting?
- Time for participants to gather relevant information?
- Available participants to attend?

If you cannot say "yes" to all of these questions, cancel, or postpone the meeting. If you proceed, you can expect disagreements, confusion, and inefficiency—magnified by the urgency of a rush meeting. Here some instances when you do not need to call a meeting because there are easier ways to share information.

- When the information is simple.

- When you need to gather simple answers.

- When you need to distribute information but do not need a response.

- When there is no time to discuss or debate an issue or problem.

- When you are more persuasive on paper than you are in person. (We'll help you improve your persuasive power in a personal meeting situation later in the book.)

The following situations would require a meeting, although you still need to evaluate costs.

- You need interaction, discussions, or opinions from other people.

- You need a group or team of employees to accomplish something.

- When the subject matter is complicated and needs to be explained.

- Finally, when your boss says you need a meeting. That simply means you need to prepare an effective meeting.

Hidden Agendas

Some people use meetings to delegate their responsibilities and lighten their work load. This is NOT an acceptable reason for a meeting. Are you the kind of person who hates creating memos and reports? That is NOT a good reason for a meeting. Do you want the business to buy lunch for you and some friends? Obviously, not a valid reason.

Count the costs, evaluate other ways to handle the project or situation, and only hold a meeting when it is the BEST answer.

WHAT CONSTITUTES A MEETING?

A meeting has specific content and a purpose that determines who should attend, what needs to be discussed, and how the information is presented. Other considerations that bear on a meeting's success are the date, time, place, and whether people need to be face-to-face or conference electronically.

There are many types of meetings that we will discuss in Chapter 2. The type you choose will depend on the people, the content, the process to be used, and the purpose. Here are other definitions of a meeting.

- A meeting is a collaborative work in process.

- It is a gathering of three or more people sharing common objectives where communication (oral or written) is a way to achieve those objectives.

The idea of having "a common objective" will be valuable to you when we discuss the what, who, and where of your meetings in Chapter 3.

WHAT MAKES A MEETING EFFECTIVE?

This is a short section, but the message is critical for anyone who plans, conducts, or attends a meeting. An effective meeting can achieve the objectives in minimal time and satisfy the maximum number of participants.

WHAT ARE THE SIGNS OF A GOOD MEETING?

These are some of the positive effects of a successful meeting.

- The opportunity to share important information with key employees and to allow for interaction and discussion with others in the meeting.

- Employees can ask questions and you can answer them. It gives you the chance to see the employees' perspective on issues.

- It is a great opportunity to direct employees in joint projects. Use the chance to watch how your employees work, talk, and interact with each other in a group.

- Important issues can be discussed with everyone in one location. This is also an ideal time to discuss and identify problems that affect employees.

- You can use the time to teach employees how to work through a problem.

- Learn about employee's experiences and help everyone learn more from them.

- Meetings that encourage participation and share information can help your employees work and feel more like a team or community.

- Effective meetings give you a chance to demonstrate and improve your leadership skills.

Keep in mind that you have the power and ability to make the meeting a flop or a success. All the information you need to plan and conduct successful meetings is contained in this book.

WHY INCLUDE ADDITIONAL PEOPLE IN THE PROCESS?

A real benefit of a properly handled meeting is the dynamic that evolves. Brainstorming sessions are fun and can be done well only in a meeting setting. E-mail is an alternative, but it slows down momentum and productivity. A well-planned meeting with the right people can reveal new alternatives and solutions that you would probably never find by yourself. A meeting allows you to include different people with various backgrounds and perspectives to increase the creative and productive potential for the group's project. We will discuss this in more detail with examples in Chapter 2.

WHAT ARE THE SIGNS OF A BAD MEETING?

Complaints people have about meetings include:

- They are not planned properly

- The wrong people are in attendance

- The right people are not included

- There is no real reason for the meeting

- The same things could be accomplished through other means

Unfortunately, there are many indicators of a bad meeting. These are some examples of things that happen at a bad meeting.

- People do not show up, arrive late, or leave early.

- Meetings become redundant and cover the same issues repeatedly without reaching a conclusion or accomplishing anything.

- Some people doze off, doodle, or have private conversations.

- The meeting goes on too long, does not accomplish everything, and people leave expressing relief that it is finally over. (It is really a bad sign when attendees are happy to get back to work!)

- Meetings are sometimes dominated by one and two people, and others are not encouraged to participate.

- People take everyone's time talking about unrelated information or they launch personal attacks on others.

Experienced meeting conductors know that there are many reasons that meetings can go bad. Here are some of the common reasons that problems arise in meetings.

- Held for wrong reasons or no reason

- Held in the wrong place and an inconvenient time

- Little or no preparation, and the participants do not understand their roles

- The leader has an ulterior (usually personal) motive for calling the meeting

In Chapter 7 we will discuss the proper way to start a meeting because a bad beginning is hard to overcome. These are some of the problems you can encounter before the meeting even begins.

- One person tries to handle everything

- Participants are not focused and do not become involved

- Employees may have low expectations or bad attitudes

Or problems may crop up during the meeting. Here are some examples.

- The conductor does not get the meeting focused or keep it focused

- The meeting drags on without accomplishing anything, possibly because of distractions or attendees' dodging responsibilities and refusing to contribute anything.

The end of your meeting needs to be handled correctly. We will discuss that in more detail in Chapter 14, but here are some examples of problems with the conclusion.

- The meeting may end suddenly with no closure and no one is sure if anything was accomplished.

- No commitment was reached and there is no call to action.

- Participants are not sure what needs to be done.

- Participants feel let down and ignored even after participating.

In Chapter 15, we will discuss following up after the meeting and collecting feedback from the participants. Here are some reasons that problems develop after a meeting is over.

- People are assigned projects and responsibilities but do not follow through.

- Past meetings were handled badly: nothing was accomplished and people assume the same thing will happen again. Did the conductor do anything to change this opinion?

- There are many repercussions from bad meetings affecting this meeting, you, and your employees.

Bad meetings can be bad for your career which is reason enough to compel you to read the rest of this book.

ARE YOU SURE YOU NEED A MEETING?

When you are deciding whether you need to call a meeting, list your goals or objectives, making it obvious whether to have a meeting, what to discuss, and whom to invite.

Ask yourself these questions:

1. Is time of the essence?
   _____ yes _____ no

2. Are the people to be involved scattered geographically?

   _____ yes _____ no

3. How many people need to attend and is it feasible?

   _____ yes _____ no

4. Does everyone need to understand the information?

   _____ yes _____ no

5. Will the information be used for reference at a later time?

   _____ yes _____ no

Or

1. Are there a number of people who have the information that is needed to make a good decision? _____ yes _____ no

2. Do you need several people to commit to the project to get the results you need and to implement the plan? _____ yes _____ no

3. Will the group dynamic help you reach a quality decision?

   _____ yes _____ no

4. Will the people in attendance have conflicting thoughts and suggestions that need to be discussed and resolved?

   _____ yes _____ no

5. Is there a concern about the fairness of the subject?

   _____ yes _____ no

These are just some of the questions to be considered when you make the decision about whether to hold a meeting or to convey the information using another option.

CASE STUDY

Meetings

While meetings may be seen as a "business thing," there are many groups and organizations that need to hold them; charities, voluntary groups, social groups, and even families may benefit from taking a structured approach to meetings.

A meeting should be held if you have a number of people who need to discuss something and make a decision. If the decision has already been made and information is just being handed down from on high, there are more efficient ways of doing this than gathering people together in one place and lecturing them. If you do not want feedback or alterations to the plan, do not hold a meeting. Send out a letter instead.

People attending your meeting should have shared goals, intentions, issues, and information about the topic well in advance, so that their responses will be ready. If you have any kind of constitution for your organization, you need to make sure that the people present are mandated to vote and that you have a sufficient number of people attending to make the decisions in question. Some constitutions require a specific number of key persons to be present, especially if the constitution itself is being amended. Checking this out in advance can save a lot of time and trouble. Be sure you know exactly what powers the meeting as a collective body possesses and do not waste time on things you are not empowered to change. If you need to include more people than will have time to speak, refine your subject, reconsider your people, and rethink the whole idea of scheduling a meeting.

Good management of time and the subject under discussion is essential. Set the time allowed for discussing a certain topic in advance. Consider setting limits on how long an individual participant may speak. Make sure whoever chairs the meeting will keep people on track both in terms of time and subject. Wandering off the topic frustrates participants, muddies issues, and wastes time. It may prevent you from making key decisions or covering all necessary topics. In an ideal world, "one subject = one meeting" has a lot of advantages, but if you have to gather people from across any geographical distance, limitations may not be practical.

Take into account how far people are traveling. If you hold a meeting of employees during work hours, all well and good, although the time could be spent working. Is a meeting the best value for your money? If you have to bring people in from a distance, incurring travelling costs, make sure you have a good reason to do so. A friend of mine recently travelled to a meeting several hours' drive away, only to find nothing was said that could not have been handled by telephone. Meetings can be a fabulous way to throw away time and money if you are not focused or have not considered cheaper and quicker alternatives.

If you have done a good job of organizing your meeting and inviting the relevant people, all should have something to say on the subject. If they do not, why are they present? Budget time for each person to speak and make sure they know in advance that you want to hear their opinion. People who are alerted about the topic under discussion and their being required to contribute are much more likely to comply. Most people do not think well on the spur of the moment and are reluctant to express themselves if they are unsure of what may be required.

To encourage participants to speak freely, set up round or square seating layouts to suggest no particular hierarchy exists. If the room layout seems to give dominance to one person or group or creates a confrontational environment (e.g., putting a desk between the organizers and other participants), people will be discouraged from speaking. If people are slow to respond, ask them open ended questions such as, "How would this affect you?" or "Can you see any issues with this?" or "Have we missed anything?" Avoid questions that suggest the answer you want to hear, such as "You will be able to implement this in a week, right?" implicitly encouraging the respondent to agree. "How soon can you implement this?" should get you a more accurate answer. If people in your meeting feel that you want to hear their honest opinions, you are much more likely to generate useful and productive responses.

Bryn Colvin
Meeting Organizer and Participant in the Voluntary Sector
http://bryncolvin.mysite.orange.co.uk

2

TYPES OF MEETINGS

———

The first "type" of meeting involves content and purpose. The second "type" of meeting pertains to how the meeting is conducted, including in person, by phone, or online. We will discuss both types in detail and which to use, depending on the meeting's purpose.

MOLD YOUR MEETING TO FIT THE PURPOSE

The purpose and goal determine how the meeting is prepared, handled, and executed. Some meetings require many people, while others are more effective with fewer participants. Consider the goals for your meeting and determine which format is better for each of your various meetings.

Elements of Meeting	Informational Meeting	Decision Making Meeting
How many people should attend?	No limit to the number	Usually 10-30 – or fewer
Who should attend?	People who "need to know"	People who can contribute
How to communicate?	Leader talk to attendees	Interactive participation
How to set up room?	Attendees face front	Participants face each other
Leadership style needed?	Authoritative leader	Encourage Participation
What to emphasize?	Focus on content	Focus on problem solving
What is the key?	Prepare information to be shared	Less formal open discussion

The goal of most meetings is to disburse information or to solve a problem, but there are variations on these purposes. The chart above will give you some specifics about the differences.

After you determine whether your meeting should dispense information or solve a problem, decide which of the following meetings you need to prepare.

Problem Solving Meeting

There are signs that changes need to be made, arising from management, clients, or employees. For these meetings to be successful, two things must happen: attendees must understand that there is a problem and they must agree that changes are needed. If your participants do not agree, they will not be helpful or productive in a meeting.

Choose people who understand a change is needed and who have the power and authority to make the change happen or find ways to convince participants before the meeting that a problem exists and things need to change. You may need financial statistics, testimonials from clients or employees, instructions from supervisors, or other persuasive information.

Decision Making

There are times in any business when decisions need to be made. Sometimes you have multiple choices and sometimes you need to create the choices and turn them over to a group for a decision. If you are seeking answers, you need to set a problem-solving meeting as explained above.

When the people who have authority to make decisions want input from employees, include those employees who have the influence to give feedback for consideration. In most cases management has definite opinions on where the useful feedback should originate, but you should be mindful that useful input can come from *anyone* in a business or organization. The person who helped Bill Gates realize he should become involved with the Internet was a young employee who saw his friends using it for more than research. You never know who in the company will have the perspective to make the right decisions.

Decision-making meetings should usually involve fewer than 15 people, but you should not go above 30. Having more people will actually prevent a decision from being made. Choose your attendees carefully and outline the steps to reach a decision before the meeting begins. There is no reason to waste time with details that should be clearly outlined before the meeting begins. Here are the elements of a decision making meeting.

1. Fully explain the problem.

2. Discuss it.

3. Explain what should be accomplished in the meeting.

4. Establish criteria to be used to evaluate alternatives.

5. Discuss possible solutions.

6. Make decisions about the alternatives.

Planning Meetings

One reason for planning meetings is to head off anticipated problems. The same principles apply to a planning meeting as a problem solving meeting so you can use much of the information discussed above. There are three types of planning meetings.

- Short-Term Plans

- Long-Term Goals

- Long-Term Problem-Solving

Short-term planning meetings should require only a few people. Long-term planning may require more people because there are more duties to be handled.

Meetings for Reporting and Making Presentations

These kinds of meeting are often misused and overused. Merely distributing reports and presentations to pertinent people may suffice.

Management might want you to verify that certain work is being done so that you call a reporting meeting to verify what is being done and who is performing the work. The participants report progress to you that you relay to management. Doing more is probably a waste of time unless you are searching for problems. If so, ply your information from smaller groups. A qualified person needs to facilitate any question and answer session to keep the meeting focused. Another person should be assigned to record all problems and other important details as they are discussed.

Some facilitators avoid staff participation, thus calling into question the reason for having a meeting. Attendees need to be encouraged to ask questions and to share their thoughts. Be sure that a qualified person is there to answer questions about the report, someone who will avoid sweeping comments or answers that discourage discussion and participation. Handled properly, question and answer sessions can give you valuable information to add to the report. After the meeting, responses should be compiled and recorded.

"React and Evaluate" Meetings

Asking for people's opinions, thoughts, and suggestions can produce valuable information and opportunities for attendees to hear the others' ideas and for you to discover the perceptions of others through their participation.

Feedback meetings need to be well planned and organized. You need a qualified facilitator to oversee them and keep participants involved and focused on the subjects at hand. It is easy for these feedback discussions to get off track. The facilitator need only guide the meeting and keep participants on the subject. When comments are negative, you cannot take it personally or be defensive. Remember, you asked for the opinions, and some people will not agree with the information being presented.

A qualified person should record details of the meeting right away and produce a written record that will settle disputes about what was said. Use these notes to create a memo to circulate to attendees.

Meetings that Focus on Multiple Tasks

Some meetings contain some reporting, a presentation, some problem solving, and decision making. Whenever a meeting shifts to a different type of procedure, it needs to be handled in an appropriate manner.

These shifts need to be handled smoothly, or attendees will be confused and miss important parts of the meeting. It is good to have a facilitator who is prepared to shift from one process to another.

Nominal Group

This is a structured meeting where attendees submit their individual ideas in writing and they are then reported to the group. This process can encourage participation from the largest number of participants. Use it when participants are familiar with the information and can offer useful input. Brainstorming is more productive when people need more information to give their comments.

Here is the nominal group process.
The facilitator poses a question and asks for suggestions.

1. Each person composes suggestions and ideas.
2. A report of the ideas is created and shared with the group.
3. After comments are shared, participants may build on them.
4. These steps can be repeated until all ideas are elicited.

Brainstorming Meetings

You can accomplish more with two or more people *working together*. This is especially true when the right people are on the same team with a strong leader. The more people you include in a planning meeting or discussion, the stronger the leader needs to be.

Feedback and suggestions from multiple people will enable you to evaluate positive and negative aspects of any situation. When the situation is complex, you need to involve more people whose perspectives can be valuable to you. Choose participants carefully and include people with different specialties. What are the concerns you need to address and who will provide useful input? Those are the people you need to invite.

You need practical and analytical people, but do not overlook creative people because after the problem is identified, you need to develop a plan. I often tell clients that coming up with the initial ideas is only the first step. After you have the idea or a possible solution, the hard work starts. How will it be implemented? Creative individuals supply the imagination and innovation to make the idea work.

The beauty of bringing the right people together to brainstorm is that a well chosen group of ingenious people is able to achieve more when you combine their abilities.

Here are the steps to brainstorm.

1. Facilitator lists all ideas on a display board .
   (The ideas should not be critiqued.)

2. Be sure that everyone in attendance understands the suggestions.

3. If duplicate ideas are offered, write them down and sort them out later.

4. Encourage people to give any suggestions that come to mind.

5. If you feel that you have all the ideas, let it rest and ask for more suggestions a little later, or if the participants are coming up with a lot of ideas, keep going. You can sort through and eliminate useless ideas later.

TECHNOLOGICAL OPTIONS FOR COMMUNICATION

The meetings discussed in the first part of this chapter are usually conducted with people seated face to face in a room. However, there is a wealth of other arrangements when you need to meet with people.

E-Mail

E-mail is a great way to send announcements, distribute information, or request that people send their thoughts about particular questions or concerns. You can also conduct a serial meeting through e-mail. All participants can share information, thoughts, opinions, and suggestions. It is a way to circulate your questions and give people a chance to think about the answers before responding.

E-mail is free and so easy to use that people use it too frequently. In years past if we received a letter, we might respond once, but you can send trivial e-mails back and forth for hours. It is more practical to send an e-mail only when you have something useful to say. Think before sending. I know that I think of something I forgot after I send many e-mails. Rushing to respond only results in more messages.

Choose E-Mail over Phone or Postal Mail

The two main reasons to use e-mail are cost savings and convenience. These are some of the main differences between e-mail and postal mail:

- E-mail is faster, but you cannot retrieve it. Be sure before you click "send."

- E-mail is free.

- E-mail is simple.

- E-mail is not private.

- E-mail can be sent to many people at one time.

- E-mail may contain typos and misspellings, since many e-mails are sent in a hurry.

E-mail Etiquette: here are some e-mail tips.
- Avoid "flaming," a personal attack through words whether spoken, written, or typed.

- Delete irrelevant information. When you respond to an e-mail, include only the relevant parts of the message. Use a descriptive subject for your message. When you respond to an e-mail, the subject line should remain the same and will be preceded by "RE:" However, when the subject of any e-mail changes, it is good to change the subject line. You will find this useful when you are reviewing saved e-mails to find something specific.

- Be clear and careful. Be sure you understand the message before you respond.

- DO NOT USE ALL CAPS. It is perceived as yelling.

Common E-mail Mistakes to Avoid:

1. Typing the message in the subject line instead of in the body.

2. Using imprecise language that can be misinterpreted.

3. Not signing off before leaving the computer, allowing others to use your e-mail address.

4. Not checking e-mail thoroughly and missing something important.

5. Forgetting your password.

6. Sending messages to the wrong e-mail address.

E-mail meetings allow each participant to have a written copy of all suggestions, questions, and ideas. Here are some things to remember with your e-mail meeting contributions:

- Keep your posts short. Short sentences and paragraphs can be read quickly.

- Focus on only one subject per message and use an appropriate subject line.

- List your name at the beginning of each post so there is no confusion about who submitted the idea.

- Your comments should be at the top of the page, not worked into the existing text.

A nice thing about e-mail meetings is that almost everyone is familiar with how they work. Remember that some people check their e-mail infrequently, and you may need to be patient with them. If you would like a simple way to notify people that they have e-mail, you can download **www.eprompter.com**, a great little program that checks all your e-mail accounts every 15 minutes and notifies you when there are messages. It is especially useful when you have more than one account to monitor.

If some participants are hesitant to join in the discussion, the facilitator should send them a reminder to nudge them to get involved. Other participants may respond to every message sent, but do not let their excessive activity mask the fact that others may not be participating.

E-mail borders on technical composition. Since you are only sending words, your meaning may be misunderstood. This is another reason to keep your messages to one subject and your answers simple. Emoticons should be avoided.

When some of your participants are concerned about getting their point across in writing, encourage them simply to state what is on their mind. They do not need to get fancy with their wording. The encouraging thing is that their comfort level will rise with practice.

Online Message Groups and Instant Messaging

Yahoo and Google offer free message boards that can be used for meetings, posting messages and reports, pictures, and graphs. The service you use depends on what you need to accomplish. On a regular basis I schedule time with business acquaintances to "chat" on Yahoo message boards, allowing each of us to read each other's comments and to share our thoughts. These boards keep the messages posted so others can read the comments when time allows. You can join free online groups at **http://groups.yahoo.com** and **http://groups.google.com/**.

You do not need any technical knowledge to establish or monitor message boards. Anyone familiar with the Internet can set one up.

Here are some sites for information about free forums:

- **www.freeforums.com**
- **www.forumco.com**
- **www.ezboard.com**
- **www.freewebspace.net/forums**
- **www.chatarea.com**
- **www.forumsservice.com**
- **www.forumforfree.com**

Forums can help you keep in touch with your employees. You can distribute business memos and newsletters on your board.

Yahoo, MSN, and AOL Messengers can be downloaded at:

- **http://messenger.yahoo.com/** - Yahoo
- **http://get.live.com/messenger/overview** – MSN
- **http://www.aim.com/** – AOL

There are other services; those are just some of the most popular. Here are some free Online Chat Services:

- **http://www.bravenet.com/webtools/chat/**
- **http://www.thefreesite.com/Free_Chat_Services/**
- **http://chat-forum.com/**
- **http://www.freebielist.com/chat.htm**
- **http://freechat.raidersoft.com/**
- **http://www.ukchatterbox.co.uk/**

Each of these services is free and some offer upgrades. You can try a free service and make sure it will work with your employees and managers. If it does, you can stick with the free service or upgrade to other options. It is better to upgrade after you determine your actual needs.

Message or discussion reports are helpful for ongoing projects or for a group working together on a regular basis. Although it slows the exchange of ideas, the group may agree up front or later whether one person will approve messages to censor fluff and delete any inappropriate posts.

Virtual Meeting Options

Even though virtual meetings do not draw people to one physical location, they are still meetings. They include people, content, and a set purpose; the location and procedure are just different, but the great advantage is flexibility: a virtual meeting can be defined as communication and collaboration among people in various locations.

Virtual meetings allow visual collaboration with others through text and images (still pictures or video). Let us discuss some of the options that virtual meetings offer you.

In the last chapter we discussed how much meetings cost. Here are some financial advantages of virtual meetings:

- There are no travel, accommodation, and meal expenses
- Work does not have to be interrupted to make a specific meeting time
- Workers lose less time and, therefore, are more productive

Virtual meetings can also bring people together who would not ordinarily be able to meet, those in other areas and time periods or those who work different shifts.

Virtual meetings encourage focus, discipline, and better use of time, eliminating the need to socialize or to be accommodating to others during the program.

There are disadvantages to virtual meetings. Some employees may not respond if the information is not delivered in person. The number of attendees will fluctuate depending on the intricacies of technology used. We'll discuss those technologies in the following section.

Audio Conferencing

The most common terminology is conference calling that enables three or more people to meet by phone or through the Internet from various locations. It saves time and money, the set up is simple, and people who are not technologically savvy can use it.

When you prepare for a conference call, you need to e-mail or fax the agenda and any report or files before the call begins. It is important to be prepared to communicate clearly during a conference call since you will not be able to see each other. All attendees should call about five minutes early to be sure they are connected before the meeting is scheduled to start. Calling late and having problems can be disruptive for everyone. Remember time zones as you notify each attendee about the meeting time.

It is best to add time to your agenda for possible delays or equipment problems. There may not be any, but it is better to be prepared. Each person on the call needs to take precautions to keep the area around them quiet and free of distractions as a courtesy to other people on the call. I've been on conference calls when I could hear children or pet noises in the background. These distractions would not happen in a business setting, but more people work from home offices today. Another possible distraction is a person using a speakerphone, a wonderful aid during a telephone conference involving a group on one end, but make sure acoustics in the room do not cause feedback or other problems. If so, have the person turn off the speakerphone or change locations.

When your conference begins, have each person identify themselves and if there are any strangers in the group, introduce them to the group. It takes little effort to create that "team" or "community" feeling when the participants are not in the same room, and introductions are a good way to test the line quality without using "testing 1, 2, 3 ..." which distracts everyone.

When you fax or e-mail information to participants before a meeting, include a list of each person involved in the conference call. Some groups who will conference call on a regular basis may exchange photos for a visual aid.

Here is a sample idea for how to conduct the meeting.

- Review the agenda, goals, and objectives for the meeting.

- Discuss any guidelines for the call including how to speak up and ask questions.

- Identify yourself in a way that identifies you and your position to the group.

- Take breaks from time to time to let people ask questions. This also gives people time to take notes.

- It is best for everyone to keep their comments brief and give others a chance to ask questions if they need more information.

- Be sure to send any notes or visual aids and let the participants know when you are referring to them.

- Speak clearly. Your voice is all the attendees have; you need to make sure they can hear and understand you.

As the conductor of the meeting you should involve everyone, making it clear who should speak and when to avoid having several people speak at once. You can ask specific people a question because they may hesitate to participate otherwise. It is helpful to explain any silence, keeping people from being distracted by the lull.

After the meeting ask people what worked for them and what did not to help you make the next conference smoother and more effective. Participants can send their comments by e-mail or fax.

You should send the minutes from the meeting to each attendee. They can be posted easily on the message boards I mentioned earlier. You could start a file for each meeting uploading any reports, graphs, agendas, photos, or minutes for convenient reference.

Teleconferencing

Teleconferencing means having interactive communication with a group of people in various areas. Participants can share information through audio, data, and video conferencing.

Multimedia conferencing is the commonly used term for a conference that uses three or more types of technology. Web conferencing is another term that is used to describe audio, data, or video conferencing that is done over the Web. High bandwidth Internet connections are also critical to keep the meeting moving at a reasonable speed. If you plan to use either of these terms, be sure that the participants agree on the details of how the conference will be handled.

Data Conferencing

The participants can share data for their meeting through whiteboards, spreadsheets, word processing programs, or graphics programs. Another option is any tools related to budgets, designs, diagrams, projections, and reports. The materials will be forwarded to the participants usually with an audio connection to facilitate discussion. The audio connection may be telephone or another audio technology.

When you prepare for a data conference, the first priority is to select someone to be in charge of technology. There are many ways to set up the equipment to complement the skills of participants. The first couple of meetings can be confusing and unproductive until the attendees are familiar with data conferencing. Therefore, it is better in the early meetings to have one person making changes to the materials. As the skills of the group members improve, things can be handled differently.

The facilitator needs to take time to become familiar with the technology before the meeting so that the meeting will run smoothly and be more productive with few distractions and interruptions.

Ask that attendees be in place 10 minutes early. An experienced technician should be on hand especially for the first couple of meetings. As the meeting facilitator, you should have files loaded and ready beforehand, demonstrating to the participants that you are a competent leader.

Take a few minutes before the meeting to explain the technology to the attendees. Be sure they know how to use it to cut down on interruptions. Be ready to step in to help or take over for another participant who may have problems.

There is a rhythm to a successful meeting. Participants should have a chance to comment and ask questions. As with any meeting, participants need to evaluate the meeting content, but also how well the technology worked and ways to improve the next meeting.

Video Conferencing

The easiest type of video conferencing occurs when meeting participants are in two or more locations and they can use video, audio, and data capabilities. Video conferencing is like an actual meeting where the participants are face to face in the same room. However, the facilitator needs to keep in mind that participants may feel uncomfortable until they are familiar with the technology.

The number of participants for a video conference should be kept to a minimum; fewer than eight people at each site is recommended. When you plan the agenda, it is good to limit the scope and keep the time shorter so that attendees stay focused.

The camera needs to be positioned close to the monitor to give the impression that the participants are looking at the camera when they are actually watching the monitor. Set the output to the monitor and double check the view that other participants will see. Doing so also allows you to check the lighting and background to ensure the best picture. It is beneficial to supply individual microphones for each attendee. They should hold up any visual aids to provide the best view for other participants. Here are some tips for the actual meeting:

- Speak "to the screen" since this is what the participants will see. But do not stare at the monitor.

- Use your normal tone of voice but speak a little slower than normal.

- Any miscellaneous noises need to be kept to a minimum, including: rustling paper, tapping the table top, sneezing, coughing, burping, and talking in the background.

When the meeting is over, ask the participants what should be done to make the next meeting better. Their feedback can pertain to the meeting content and procedures. With each of these meetings, remember that you will work out the kinks and difficulties over time.

Fax and E-Mail

Fax and e-mail attachments are the simplest and quickest methods to send files. Fax has worked well for years, but e-mail attachments offer even quicker service with far better quality. When you send a file to a person for a meeting, the recipient may need to modify it. Make sure the recipients have the appropriate software or ability to modify the files you sent them. It is better to send files by e-mail, but if you need only get information to them, fax is suitable.

One possible problem with e-mail attachments is that some e-mail accounts can send and receive only smaller files. A flexible and free alternative to this problem is **www.yousendit.com** but it has limitations. You can also compress the files with a program like WinZip (**www.winzip.com**). To use WinZip, the sender and recipient must have the program and know how to use it. You may also send files on a CD by mail. Doing so takes time, money, and effort, but it does work.

3

THE WHO, WHAT, AND WHEN OF YOUR MEETING

This chapter will help you make decisions that will determine whether your meeting will accomplish its purpose.

WHO

Much of the success of your meeting depends on your choice of people to attend and the time you choose to meet. Certain times are better for meetings as you will see below. Who needs to be included on your list of people to attend your meetings? Involve as few people as possible to cause fewer distractions and less expense, but do not eliminate any participants whom you really need. If your list grows unwieldy, consider creating subcommittees.

Personalities at your meeting will have a direct impact on what happens and how much is accomplished. Here is a simple example of your choice of attendees determining the outcome. Your boss wants a group to decide whether to add new products or to cut the current line of products. If you only invite people who want to cut the product line, obviously, that will be the final decision. However, if you invite people who can offer the positive and negative side of each possibility, you have a much better chance of getting an effective result.

WHAT

What information needs to be discussed or which problems need to be solved? Making a list or an outline helps participants be prepared to stay on the subject, avoiding rambling discussions.

Do you need regularly scheduled meetings? Some businesses have meetings automatically scheduled for a specific day and time. On one job that I had meetings were scheduled each morning at 7 a.m. and 8 a.m. even if there was no known reason. They were especially irritating for staff members who worked on other floors and had to stop work, only to learn that there was nothing to discuss. It would have been more effective to cancel the meeting. rather than wasting time.

Ask yourself these questions to find whether the meeting is necessary.

- Is anything gained by holding the meeting?
- Is anything lost by not holding the meeting?
- Would an e-mail or fax accomplish the same thing?
- Could you schedule fewer meetings and accomplish just as much?
- Do participants have enough time to prepare?
- Do you really want input on the situation or problem?
- How will the meeting purpose affect the participants?

Here are some common purposes for meetings. Do any of them fit your plans?

- To give announcements and status reports
- To share results (committee reports)

- To offer presentations on subjects that will interest participants

- To coordinate projects, schedules, and group or individual assignments

- To offer training or the chance to learn new skills and procedures

- To set goals and objectives and develop strategies to accomplish them

- To solve problems, analyze issues, and ideas and discuss possible solutions

- To make decisions, evaluate situations and options and to gain a consensus

- To socialize and take time to get to know each other

- To build a team that will motivate and inspire staff members

Most meetings involve problem solving, bringing staff members together to generate ideas and find creative solutions, but your meeting can have more than one purpose. You can also incorporate ongoing purposes in your meeting. Some ongoing purposes include:

- Building a Team

- Improving Safety Practices

- Increasing Productivity

- Increasing Employee Knowledge

- Building Leadership Skills

These are only a few of the possible underlying purposes that you can incorporate into all business or departmental meetings.

A clear purpose is the first step in an effective and successful meeting.

Know Your Purpose

During a meeting have you ever asked, "Why are we here?" No doubt this question has occurred to you whenever a meeting rambles. People want to know why they are in a situation and that includes meetings. Attendees may not ask you directly, but they are probably asking themselves or other people why they are at the meeting. It is critical that you have an answer to that question. These are some examples of things you should and should NOT say to meeting attendees.

<u>Bad to Say</u>

- "We are here today since we haven't had a meeting in a long time."

- "We need to discuss a new service (or product) that we are launching tomorrow."

- "We have some ideas on ways to restructure the department and we are going to tell you what they are."

Let's reword these thoughts.

<u>Good to Say</u>

- "We are meeting because I need the details about what you are working on."

- "This meeting was called for me to tell you the details about a new product (or service) that we will launch tomorrow."

- "We are here to discuss some ideas to restructure the department, and I need your thoughts and suggestions."

Next consider whether this meeting is to get or to give information and list the information you will share. As you create the list, be realistic.

- Is the purpose something that you can accomplish?

- Do you have the information handy that the attendees need?

- Do you personally understand this information?

- Do attendees already have the information they need?

- Is there enough time to discuss and handle the subject?

- Did you invite the right people to the meeting to accomplish the purpose?

- Do you have the authority to see the purpose through to a conclusion?

- Did you invite the person who does have the authority, if you do not?

- Have you thoroughly prepared for the meeting?

Make the Purpose Known

It is human nature for our minds to wander to negative possibilities when we do not know what is happening. Therefore, attendees need to understand the purpose for the meeting, enabling them to prepare and participate more fully. When attendees do not understand the purpose and are not prepared, they may be critical of what is happening. You can eliminate this concern by being clear about the purpose for your meeting. Even when the purpose is confidential, attendees should be told something. Otherwise, you may lose control of the meeting in their rush to ask questions.

Avoid Ulterior Motives

Take a close look at your plans and purpose to ensure the agenda has no fuzzy language. Have you listed a topic, but you plan to discuss something different? A new meeting leader may be able to get away with this – once. It will make employees feel that you are unprepared or incompetent. Your more experienced staff members will spot the ploy, and it will undermine your effectiveness. When a leader is honest and direct, others are encouraged to give honest feedback and suggestions and to ask pertinent questions. You will have created an atmosphere more conducive to learning and accomplishing your tasks.

Tell Others About the Purpose

We will talk in detail about how to plan a meeting, but this section is about helping others to prepare. No matter how well you prepare, you cannot bring a cold subject to the table and expect attendees to warm to it. How can they prepare any information or prepare mentally if they do not even know what the meeting will be about? They need enough time to do any research or preparation before the meeting.

To prepare, attendees need specific information such as

- **Subject and Purpose** – You do not need to outline every single detail, but the few minutes you take to explain will save everyone's time at the meeting.

- **Supply an Agenda** – Include the specific information you plan to cover on your agenda. Forgo the drama: do not leave things off to get a reaction. Tell attendees what will be covered. When you spring unexpected topics on the participants, they will not respond positively.

We will discuss the agenda is complete detail in Chapter 5, but here are a few tips about using one. It is like a road map to get your meeting from point A to point B based on where you want to start the meeting and where you will lead the attendees. Your agenda needs to be clear, specific, and brief.

This is one example of a broad agenda item and how to make it more focused. Let us say your business wants to offer a scholarship. The agenda can say that the attendees will consider a company scholarship, or it can say that attendees will discuss how to screen applicants from three area high schools to receive a scholarship from the company. Do you see the difference in these two approaches? The more specific information will help the attendees prepare information and details that will be more helpful.

- **What Do You Expect** – Tell meeting attendees what you expect from them. If you want comments about specific agenda items, tell them ahead of time, especially true when you invite certain people for a certain reason. When you need someone to contribute to a specific topic, make this known when you invite them or when you send them a copy of the agenda. If their contribution regards research or compilation of information, they need enough time to assemble the details you need.

- **Meeting Details: When and Where** – Meeting attendees need to know when the meeting will be, where it will be, and how long it will last. This information requires advance planning to secure a site or meeting room, make sure attendees are available, and provide enough time to cover the agenda.

You want to avoid calling someone 10 minutes before the meeting start time and inviting them to be there.

When you notify attendees about the meeting, keep the following details in mind.

1. **Write it Down** – Compose and communicate. Do not expect people to remember the details. It is much more effective to fax them, send a memo, or a quick e-mail with the information.

2. **Preparation Time** – Keep in mind that business people are busy. Do not put an undue rush on attendees to prepare their contributions.

3. **Confirmation** – You, or someone helping you, should verify that all invited attendees received their notification and information about the meeting. This should take only a moment or two to confirm they received the information and read it.

It is to your advantage to do everything possible to see that all potential attendees are notified and can be prepared for your meetings.

Group Attitudes and Behaviors to Avoid

The same issues can be found when you invite only workers or supervisors. These limitations in attendees can cause dangerous mind sets that should be avoided. A biased viewpoint and contribution to the discussion can cause the group to make erroneous decisions. Psychologist Irving L. Janis calls the tendency of a group to think alike: "Groupthink." How can you make groupthink work to your advantage? Here are some tips.

1. Some meeting participants may feel they can help create a team atmosphere by agreeing with others, even if decisions do not reflect their thoughts, beliefs, and experiences. This mind-set will skew the outcome of your meetings. They may feel that stating their disagreement with others will show they are not working with the group. Make it clear that you welcome ALL viewpoints and suggestions.

2. Having a little authority goes to some people's heads. Remember that just because someone is in charge does not mean they have the right opinion. If that was the assumption, there would be no reason for a meeting with others. The "I am right" attitude can lead to disastrous problems that can be avoided through unbiased participation.

3. Some groups cling to certain thoughts, beliefs, and ideas because they have worked in the past. This means the new people are expected to leave their thoughts and beliefs at the door. This is not a productive way for a group to work and will limit the effectiveness of the group.

4. When employees are promoted they may forget what it is like to be in the lower levels of the company. Supervisors may only promote people who have similar viewpoints or who are willing to set aside their thoughts to agree with their superiors. This is another dangerous precedent and should not be encouraged. It may create networks of people who work well together, but they do not consider the needs of dissenters who may be innovative or creative.

5. Some groups just need to make a decision and will ignore people who disagree with them. In these cases the majority opinion can steamroll over the minority.

6. Meeting attendees may feel pressured to "go along" with supervisors or executives who have stated their thoughts on a subject. Supervisors and executives should participate in your meetings, but their ideas should not serve to squelch other opinions.

7. Participants may agree when under pressure to make decisions. Meetings are often conducted using different rules when there is unusual pressure to make a decision. The decisions reached in these situations may not reflect the honest feelings and beliefs of the participants.

8. After one decision is made in a group with this skewed mentality, they find it even easier to make other erroneous decisions in the same way.

All groups need to avoid these pitfalls. It is a mentality that can make your meetings ineffective no matter how much planning you do. Keep the lines of communication open with all participants and invite people who can represent each side of an issue and who will speak up with the information they can supply.

Whom to Invite

Pitfalls mentioned in the last section can be avoided by inviting a good mix of people with varied backgrounds. The more diversified the group, the fairer the meeting and the easier the evaluation should be for you. With a variety of viewpoints and backgrounds represented at the meeting, the more likely you are to hear various sides of the situation. It is also effective to include people who are actually affected by the problem that you are trying to solve.

In problem-solving meetings the attendees you choose are especially important in these meetings. You need to pick people who have information to contribute to problem solving. When you plan a meeting where you need to solicit information, pick people who can contribute to the meeting.

Here are some tips for choosing the participants for your problem solving meetings:

1. For problem solving meetings, bring people from other departments and various backgrounds to get diversified input.

2. Take advantage of the personnel resources available within the company.

3. Invite people who can help you sell the idea or explain the problem or situation to the attendees. If there is someone whose input is needed to make the meeting more effective, that person should be invited.

4. Elements and details of the problem will dictate the attendees. Bring in people with experience and knowledge in all aspects of the problem.

5. You could need input about development, marketing, production, research, and sales. Which people will have useful information? They need to be on your list.

6. Invite a good mix of supervisory people and staff members. You need input from both levels of personnel and it can be beneficial to gather input from each of these groups.

7. Invite the people most affected by the problem.

If anyone approaches you about attending the meeting, be honest with them and yourself about whether they have anything to contribute or if they will benefit in any way by attending. It can be good to explain the agenda to these people and the objectives. This should help them understand who was invited and why. These are some most common ways that they might react:

- They will agree and appreciate your consideration.

- They will disagree and list the reasons why you should change your mind.

- They will disagree, but understand you have made your decisions.

These are some of the initial criteria to use to decide who should attend your meetings.

- **Knowledge of Subject** – Participants need to have information and experience that would enable them to be a contributing participant in the meeting.

- **Committed to Finding a Solution** – Some individuals may have information that would help but do not want to put forth the effort to help the group. Take a look at the people you are considering. Do they have a vested interest in finding a solution?

- **Time Available** – Do the people you are considering have the time to attend the meeting? Some individuals are booked solid and pushed to get normal daily duties done. Be sure that you must have the person in attendance and especially if they have a jam-packed schedule.

- **Various Points of View** – Remember that you need varied points of view and opinions so that the group can consider all possibilities. Include people who are familiar with all aspects of the subject matter and include creative individuals to find ways to implement the ideas that are generated in the meeting.

- **Speak Your Mind** – The participants need to feel free to express their thoughts, opinions, and the facts about the subject. It will not help you to suppress their initiative, willingness to participate, or creativity. They need to be encouraged to get the best results.

- **Open Your Mind** – All participants need to keep an open mind. Nothing should be impossible in the opening discussions. Get as many suggestions as possible and then narrow them down. It is important that all attendees listen to each other. This is the way to get the best possible combination of input from the attendees. They also need to be willing to listen and change their mind, if it is appropriate.

You could create a chart with each of these qualities and list the potential participants. Then manually check or place an "x" beside each name to determine who should attend the meeting.

Quality	"A"	"B"	"C"	"D"	"E"	"F"
Knowledge						
Commitment						
Time						
Viewpoint						
Speak Mind						
Open Mind						

This can help you evaluate the best people to attend the meeting.

The form below could help you create your notification e-mail or fax. This is only a suggestion. Feel free to make any needed changes or adjustments to fit your needs.

MEETING MEMO	
To:	Date:
From:	
Below is the information you need for our meeting. Please let me know if you have any questions. I look forward to a productive meeting.	
Meeting Date:	Time:

Location/Directions to Meeting:
Parking or Transportation Information: (if needed)
Meeting Subject, Focus, and Purpose: (Agenda is Attached for Your Review.)
Preparation Needed from You:

Any Special Attire: (if applicable)	Meal Details: (if relevant)

When the Meeting is Out of Town	
Travel Details:	Accommodation Details:

Instructions to Submit Bills:
Travel Expenses:
Hotel Expenses:
Meal Expenses:
Parking Fees:
Please submit all expense information as soon as you return to work. We ask that you notify us about any questions and concerns about the meeting agenda attached for your review.

Categories of People to Include

There are three categories to consider: people who should attend, people whom you should think about carefully before inviting and those whose absence would cause you to consider rescheduling. Here are some details about these people.

People Who Should Attend

- People who can influence or assist the meeting to accomplish its purpose.
- People who have special interest in the subjects you will discuss.
- People with the power to approve and implement changes from meeting.
- People with particular information on your meeting topics.
- Presenters who can contribute to your meeting.
- Problem solvers or people who can find creative solutions.
- Some people may attend your meeting for additional training.

Think Carefully Before Inviting These Individuals

- People who cannot or will not contribute to the purpose.
- Disruptive people.
- People with limited interest or knowledge about the meeting topic.
- Some people would be insulted or hurt if they are not invited.

Reschedule the Meeting if These People Cannot Attend

- People opposed to the topic who need to hear the discussion.
- People who could influence the outcome of the meeting.
- If they cannot attend, try to link with them through a phone or video conference.
- Important people who need to be included but do not have time to prepare.

How Many People Should Attend

People often wonder if there is a magic number of people who should attend a meeting. That totally depends on the type of meeting being held. I provided some rough guidelines in Chapter 2 about the size of the meeting based on the type of meeting. You need enough people to accomplish your goals without having additional people just sitting around. How is that for a vague comment?

Here is some advice to help you determine the number of participants to include.

Determining How Many People Should Attend by Meeting Type	
Purpose/Type of Meeting	Number of People
Meeting with Interaction and Involvement from Participants	10 or less
Meeting to Generate Ideas and Make Decisions	5 - 8
Meeting to Communicate Information with Limited Discussion *These include: announcements, celebrations, awards, speeches, and similar events.*	10 +

Remember to use smaller groups for idea and feedback discussions. If you start out with a large group, those participants can be broken into smaller groups. These smaller groups can discuss ideas and suggestions and report to the larger group. This is a great way to use a large number of people for generating ideas and solving problems. It is good to choose the people who work together in smaller groups. There are many ways to use this meeting format.

Another option is to have a smaller meeting, before the main meeting. This would include attendees who represent the larger group. The smaller group can discuss particular details that do not need to be discussed with the entire group. It is easier to interact with the smaller group, and you will not have to tie up the large group on unnecessary details. Using this method will shorten your overall meeting time to save the company's time and money.

Part-Time Attendees

Are there attendees who do not need to be involved in the entire meeting? A great example of this is training meetings for a leadership group. In networking meetings, there can be officers who oversee various segments of the meeting. When these people are being trained, the schedule can work like this:

President – Attend entire meeting
Vice President – Attend entire meeting
Secretary/Treasurer – Attend entire meeting
Training Supervisor – Attends the portion of the meeting that involves their duties
Guest Hosts – Attends the portion of the meeting that involves their duties

The president, vice president and secretary/treasurer need to attend all sessions because any of them could be requested to conduct a meeting. The other positions only require specialized training for their particular area and that is the only sessions that they would have to attend. [This is how training sessions were handled within the Virginia Business Networking International (BNI) groups that I attended and where I filled various offices in the groups. **www.bni.com**]

Additional Considerations About Whom to Include

There may be occasions when you need an expert, someone from another business, people from the neighborhood, city of county officials, or any other people or groups who would be affected by your meeting subject. They can bring a new viewpoint and energy to the group and could be valuable in the right situation.

What should you do if you cannot find people to represent various viewpoints? You can create a list with all possible qualifications down the left side and list potential attendees across the top and indicate which person fills each vacancy. This will help you evaluate which factions you need to add.

Diversity is a necessary quality in your participants. The meeting will be energized with a group of people with different views and backgrounds. This is the energy that sparks the best ideas and is great to brainstorm ideas. A skilled facilitator is also needed to maintain order, while encouraging the productive flow of ideas. As your skills grow, you will welcome the energy and learn to use it for the benefit of the meeting. A lively group is challenging, but it is much more fun and productive.

In meetings where you need to solve a problem, inexperienced facilitators may press for a quick decision. Learn to take your time and be sure that all possibilities have been explored. Keep these things in mind:

- Take your time

- Do not push too hard

- Do not panic

- Double check the input you received

- Do not insist on a decision if there was not enough information generated

There are times when it is better to delay the final decision. You might want to let the attendees go home or back to work and think about the question privately. Then you can schedule a short meeting in a couple of days or the following week to see if there are any additional thoughts and suggestions. I find it inspiring to get out of the room and to clear my mind.

After the meeting is over, you need to be sure the attendees do not fall into a negative or passive mind set. Here are some tips to prevent this problem.

- Encourage participants to talk with others in their department before the next meeting. This can yield some wonderful suggestions.

- Post a list of the main points from the meeting for everyone to see. Invite them to submit ideas and suggestions about the details from the meeting.

- When you need approval from another group, get their input and approval (if possible) before your next meeting.

- If the decision maker cannot or will not attend the meetings, keep them updated on all information.

- When the decision is especially weighty, divide the attendees into smaller groups and review the details with different individuals. This can ensure that the participants have reviewed all sides of the situation.

Now that you know the sort of people, experience, and background that you need, let us discuss how many of these qualified people should be invited to your meeting.

How Many People to Invite

First, you need to ask yourself how many people are needed to accomplish the goals for your meeting. This is one of the reasons we discussed figuring out the purpose of your meeting first. Decide what you need to accomplish and then you are in a better position to decide who to involve and how many people to include.

Who has not suffered through a meeting that was too long? One reason for overlong meetings is poor planning, but another reason can be that too many people are included. We will discuss different size meetings and how to accomplish the most possible. There are several different numbers of people that can be included and we will review how to use each size group to your best advantage. You will find that the meeting dynamics vary depending on the number of people in attendance. Which dynamic does your meeting need? And what dynamic can you facilitate effectively?

Two to Eight Attendees

This number is appropriate for a single small department with the manager leading the meeting. Do all the people in the department need to attend staff meetings? Here are the elements that will help you make that determination.

Whenever two or more people get together, the dynamics change. Even with a small group, the meeting should be overseen, prepared, and properly executed. With fewer than five people, you probably do not need someone to facilitate the group. But someone needs to have a solid plan for what needs to be accomplished. The agenda could be circulated to each attendee, and each person can prepare information for each topic. This would give everyone a chance to participate and would take the entire burden of preparation off the shoulders of one person.

When the group is only a few people, an argument can start between two of the people. If this happens, one of the other people needs to step in and facilitate to avoid losing control of the meeting. If the group drifts off subject, someone needs to speak up to get the meeting back on track. There may be times when the meeting becomes emotionally charged or everyone is intimately involved. It is best to recess the meeting and call in a person to oversee the proceedings to give the attendees a chance to calm down before discussing the topics further.

AN ADDITIONAL TIP

With practice you will learn when to allow the meeting to run its course or when there needs to be more oversight and facilitation. There could be times when a neutral outsider needs to facilitate the meeting. You will understand how to handle various situations over time. Until you learn everyone's idiosyncrasies, try not to let the meeting get out of control, but feel free to stop the meeting if things get bad. You might want to talk with people who have been conducting meetings for a long time and get them to share tips and suggestions.

Eight to Fifteen Attendees

This is the ideal size for problem solving meetings. This number of people allows each person to participate and gives everyone a chance to hear what others think. The smaller size also gives you the option to keep the meeting informal. It is fine to be informal, but you still need a clear purpose and structure for the most effective meeting. If you have a standard agenda template, make changes to have time to focus on the more important aspects.

Fifteen to Thirty Attendees

You do not need this many people for most meetings. Remember, the dynamics of the group change when you include more than 15 people. When you have this many attendees, problem solving potential is diminished and participation must be limited. However, if you want to share information, this many attendees might be best. The meeting facilitator must have sufficient experience to handle a larger group and certain rules must be set and enforced.

More than Thirty Attendees

Large groups are best for lectures, panel discussions, formal debates, and conducting a vote. If people are going to participate, there must be rules and they must be enforced. Parliamentary procedure is usually best suited for large groups. Earlier we discussed the possibility of breaking large meetings into smaller groups to gather problem solving feedback. When you decide to do this, have definite suggestions about how the small groups will operate and what they need to accomplish. An experienced facilitator should also roam among the participants to ensure they accomplish things and to answer questions that might arise.

WHEN

The right meeting time can make a big difference in the attendance, the participation, and the productivity of your meeting. Some days of the week are also better for meetings. I've found that Mondays and Fridays have never been good for me. These are some things you need to consider.

- When are you available?

- When will you be thoroughly prepared?

- When are your participants available?

- When can your participants be available?

- When is the meeting place available, whether in your building or somewhere else?

- How long will it take to prepare the meeting area?

Some of the worst times to conduct meetings, include late afternoons before holidays or weekends and early mornings after holidays or weekends.

A meeting during lunch with brown bags or a catered lunch with deli sandwiches or a breakfast of donuts, pastries, coffee, and juice might be a solution. Many groups meet before or after business hours. This is especially true with civic and professional organizations. It can be challenging to find a suitable meeting time for a large group of professionals. Weekday evenings are some of the only possibilities. Some groups may even need to meet on Saturday morning or Sunday afternoon. No time is unacceptable if the facility is available and the attendees are in agreement. You can use a day planner to figure which days or time would be better for your meeting. It might be better to make photo copies of your calendar page to work on.

Choosing the right time for your meeting can be a trial and error situation sometimes. It is useful to evaluate the effectiveness of different meeting days and times.

CASE STUDY

I was working as the dispatcher and parts manager for Rock County TV & Appliance and Douglas Refrigeration in Janesville, Wisconsin, in the late 1980s and early 1990s. In this capacity I ran the office out of the basement of the business, answered every call for the refrigeration business, and scheduled appointments for the appliance and television techs. It meant that the phones started ringing at 7:30 a.m. and did not stop until 5:30 p.m.

Inevitably there was an all-store business meeting planned about once a month. Even though I started out attending, I usually ended up either answering the phones on the first floor or going down to the basement so that I could check schedules or help customers with getting their parts, as the meeting was usually set at 8 a.m.

I always found out what went on from one of my co-workers, but it would have been much better if these meetings would have been set for just before opening so that everyone could attend.

Sherry Wille writing as Sherry Derr-Wille & Shari Dare
www.derr-wille.com

INITIAL PLANNING FOR YOUR MEETING

Earlier in this book, we discussed how important it is to properly plan and prepare your meetings. Planning is broken into three chapters and this is the first chapter that deals with how to plan. In Chapter 5 we will discuss how to plan your agenda. And Chapter 6 will discuss strategic planning.

BEGIN TO PLAN

I have included several series of questions and checklists to help you with the initial planning stages for your meeting. Let us start with the simplest worksheet.

MEETING PLANNING WORKSHEET
Objective
What do you want and need to accomplish in the meeting?

Meeting Length

How long does your meeting need to be?

When should it be held?

What day and time would be best?

Attendees

Who needs to be included? Include people in authority, people committed to finding a solution, and people who need to know the information.

Agenda

What individual things will be discuss or present?

Who will plan the agenda?

Who will distribute the agenda?

Will participants contribute to agenda?

Meeting Location

What sort of location and equipment are needed?

What type of layout would be best for your meeting?

Individual Roles

What roles will attendees play in the meeting? This includes: facilitator recorder, secretary, and speaker.

Follow-up

How will you gather feedback from attendees?

How will you evaluate the effectiveness and success of your meeting?

These points include basic information that you need to prepare for your meeting. Some have already been discussed and the other items will be discussed later in the book. However, this list puts the basics in front of you and helps you know where to start.

Detailed Steps to Plan Meeting

To plan an effective meeting, you need to understand the elements that your meeting needs. It is important that you understand each of these elements to y plan an effective meeting. These are the 15 steps that should be used to take your meeting from preparation to conclusion and evaluation. Additional questions and points are listed along with each step in the planning process to help you prepare your plan more thoroughly.

1. **Determine the Purpose and Desired Outcome** – What points will be discussed or presented at the meeting? What do you need to accomplish? What decisions or actions should result from the meeting?

2. **Establish Boundaries for the Meeting** – Establish your objectives and then decide how the meeting will begin and end. Will there be an indication that the objective has been met?

3. **Determine the Meeting Objectives** – Pick three to six goals based on the meeting purpose. What actions need to be taken to accomplish these goals?

4. **Owner** – Who will be responsible to see that the goals are met? Who will oversee the project? What happens if the goals are not met?

5. **Choose Effective Agenda Points** – Choose the main things that must be done to accomplish these goals.

6. **Process the Necessary Information** – Do you have access to the information that you need? Does it need to be organized? Do you need assistance to organize the materials? What is the proper procedure to assemble the information?

7. **Choose the Effective Tools to be Used** – What tools will be used to assemble the information?

8. **Take Responsibility** – Someone needs to be responsible for each item in the meeting that requires action. At times you only need an individual, but at other times you need to assign a task to a group. Evaluate how many people are needed and find the appropriate people or person to handle each item.

9. **What is the Time Frame for the Meeting** – Each item on your agenda should have a specific time frame. Determine how much time will be needed to effective cover each item and allocate that amount of time.

10. **What Roles are Needed and Who Will Fill Them** – Who will be the meeting: leader, facilitator recorder, presenter, and participants? Do you need to fill each of these roles? In a smaller meeting you do not need to assign each of these roles. Who will fill these roles and what responsibilities do they have? Who needs to attend and how many people will you include?

11. **Establish the Logistical Needs for Your Meeting** – Decide on the location, time, and day for the meeting. This should also include information about how long the meeting will last. Consider any other company events such as vacations when you determine the date and time.

12. **Assemble the Needed Materials** – What materials are needed? These materials could include handouts, charts, graphs, chalk boards, whiteboards, and projectors. How should the materials be presented to maximize their effectiveness for the attendees? Does the facility you have chosen offer the possibilities that you need? If not, an adjustment in location or materials must be made.

13. **Establish Appropriate and Necessary Ground Rules** – The "ground rules" include: behavior expectations, procedures, performance, and evaluation. The attendees need to agree on the ground rules before the meeting begins. If needed, you can list

the rules on a piece of paper and have each attendee sign the sheet to indicate that they are in agreement.

14. **Acceptable Actions** – Must agree on the steps to be taken, how to develop a plan of action, planning any additional meetings, and any necessary changes in the way business is done. It is critical that everyone understands what needs to be done and who is responsible for what.

15. **Perform a Follow-Up Evaluation** – Attendees need to evaluate the meeting, the flow of information, the various roles, how they were handled, and the outcome of the meeting. Evaluations should not just indicate there are problems but suggestions on how to improve future meetings.

These individual elements of your meeting will be discussed in more detail as you read this book.

Collect, Organize, and Present Data

After you establish the purpose of the meeting, you need to determine what tools and procedures are needed to accomplish that purpose. Here are some particular things to include:

- Have you acquired the data you need?

- Are there enough data available?

- Are all aspects of the subject covered by the data?

- Do you need to assign someone to collect more data? Whom should you pick?

- What additional information do you need?

- What do the data reveal to you?

- What tools or procedures should be used to collect the data?

<u>Organize</u>

- Have you organized the data?

- Will it be useful to the attendees as it is, or does it need to be reorganized?
- How can it be organized better?
- What do the data reveal?
- How should you organize the data?

Compile

- Has the information been compiled?
- Is it usable or should it be compiled in a different way?
- Is the compilation clear to others?
- How could it be made clearer?
- What procedure should be used to compile the information?

Sequence

- What sequence is indicated?
- Do you have specific steps, phases, levels, stages established for the data?
- Can it be organized better?

Break It Down

- Can the information be managed in large groups of data?
- Does it need to be broken down?
- What would be the best way to break it down?
- What will make it more usable?
- Are the data presented in the simplest manner?
- Would the data reveal more if they was broken down further?

<u>Map the Information</u>

- Do participants need to understand the flow and compilation of the data?

- Is it possible to map the flow of information to make it understandable?

- Would it be better if the data were mapped?

- What mapping process would make it easier to understand and use?

- What could the information tell you with thorough mapping?

<u>Display</u>

- Would a display make it easier for attendees to understand?

- Can it be displayed to make it easier to break down?

- Does the display make the correlation more clear?

- Are the data displayed in a useful manner?

- Could they be changed to make them more useful?

- What does the display tell the meeting participants?

Every question will not apply, but many will help you to evaluate elements of your meeting in more detail. You can also feel free to add more information and questions that come to you while you are working. I've found it useful to customize forms and questionnaires with specific information that is helpful to me. You might want to do the same. Keeping the details and questions in a word processing file makes it easy to make adjustments to suit your own style.

PREPARE FOR YOUR MEETING

Have you been to meetings where the conductor stumbles over his words? What about participants who shuffle their papers but do not seem to know what to say? These actions are common. Advance preparation would solve this problem. Everyone who attends the meeting should prepare before the meeting. This is especially true for the conductor and participants. The meeting can become disorganized quickly when people are not prepared.

When this happens, it is a waste of time and money for the participants and the company that is paying for the meeting.

Another problem is a meeting with an incomplete or loose agenda. When the conductor begins the meeting without a completed and organized agenda, the meeting will have no direction. Some of your attendees may have conducted many meetings and feel that they do not need to prepare, but each meeting should be planned in advance.

Team or Solo Preparation

Is it better to prepare for a meeting by yourself or should you work in conjunction with others? It can be easier to prepare the meeting alone, because you do not need to coordinate your efforts with someone else.

CASE STUDY

For a small group with about eight people, this is how we organize our periodic meetings. One person is assigned to be the leader and each attendee sends thoughts and problems to the leader over a four- to-eight week period.

An agenda is created using the points contributed by attendees. The various topics are then delegated to the attendee who mentioned them. Each person is expected to prepare the information needed by the group to discuss this topic. The person then presents the information to the group, under the leader's leadership. Any support documents are either furnished or brought by individuals to be distributed or read to the group when the topic is discussed.

To avoid confusion, the attendees raise their hands to be recognized by the leader. This helps the leader maintain control and keeps the meeting organized.

Richard Henkel, Business Manager; Bussey Davis and Associates

However, if it is a large or complex meeting it might be better to consult with others for help in organizing all the elements of the meeting.

These are some of the reasons you would want to include others in your preparation.

- Use their creativity and get their input on the plans and agenda.

- Portions of the preparation can be delegated to qualified people. (Do NOT delegate to unqualified or unmotivated people.)

- Attendees will feel more involved in the process and will do more to make the meeting effective.

- This can be a way to train your employees and to increase their leadership skills.

So, you know it would be good to include others in your planning, but how do you pick the right people? Here are some ideas:

- Consider their strengths and weaknesses. Do they complement you and will you work well together?

- What is their job in the company or department? Are they people who will be able to contribute additional information to the meeting?

- Evaluate their connections within the company. Who do they know and can they help you make the meeting more effective?

Even when you are considering people to help with the planning, they need to further the goals of the meeting and be qualified to help you. If they are not qualified, are they willing to learn and to do more? A willing attitude is important. After some time you will be able to identify people who will not or cannot improve. If you have been working with someone who is not improving, you should cut the ties and work with someone different. This will save frustration and wasted time for both of you.

Ground Rules

Ground rules need to be established before the meeting and all participants need to understand the rules. If not, the meeting can easily fall apart. One simple rule is that only one person should speak at a time and that people must raise their hand to speak. The conductor will then call on people to speak. These are simple things that make a big difference in how the meeting is conducted and its effectiveness.

These ground rules can also include such things as:

- Behavior of the conductor.

- Outline any specific information about behavior of the participants.

- Determine the procedure to present agenda items.

- Decide how subjects will be introduced and discussed.

- Create a procedure to collect and evaluate information.

- Decide how disruptions and problems in the meeting will be handled.

- Decide that meetings will begin and end on time.

- Decide that side issues must be handled at a different time. This will keep the meeting focused on the current subject.

- Make it known that all viewpoints are important and each person needs to be given a chance to speak. This also means that people will not be criticized for sharing their thoughts and opinions.

- It is best to collect all thoughts, ideas, and opinions first. After they are collected and possibly screened, they can be discussed.

- Make it clear that the facilitator is in charge. This is more important and necessary with larger groups because of the dynamics for these groups.

- Any decisions need to be made only with a group consensus. There can be different ways to reach a consensus and one of these should be used. These decisions need to be made by all members in the group.

- All participants need to exercise constructive skills to work together and to work toward decisions and solving problems. Much time can be wasted if participants do not work constructively to help each other reach their goals.

- It is best for presenters and speakers to prepare visual materials ahead of time and bring copies for the participants or large visual aids that can be seen by the group.

Many people refer to Robert's Rules of Order, but they may not really understand the rules or may just think they have to refer to it. Any rules that you plan to use need to be reviewed to be sure that they are effective. If you find problems, the rules need to be adjusted to make them more effective. When you consider making changes, try new rules with the group and then adopt them once you know they work.

It is better not to implement too many rules at once. Depending on your group, it could be better to introduce several rules at a time and add more over time. Too many rules at once can be overwhelming and feel like a dictatorship to the attendees. Rules are not meant to be a burden. They are meant to help you maintain order and to keep the meeting on track to be more effective.

Meeting Logistics

Logistical planning is important for your meetings, especially larger ones. Do not let yourself get caught thinking that someone else is handling it. You need to know who is handling it and ensure that everything is ready in time for the meeting. Effective meetings and good logistics do not just happen. They are a result of careful preparation.

The meeting location and layout are just the beginning because many other things need to be coordinated. Following are some things to remember.

Equipment

- It is important to be specific about the equipment you need. You might even want to submit the make and model that you prefer.

- For a presentation using PowerPoint, for example, you would probably use your own equipment.

- It is also good to have backup equipment in case there is a mechanical problem. You might want to take a few minutes to be sure that someone knows how to do simple things like check for outlets and light switches.

Visual Aids

- All handouts, displays, presentation materials, and other visual aids need to be ready and on the site before the meeting begins.

- Do NOT rely on the postal service to deliver your materials. Keep them with you or have someone that you trust deliver them.

Breaks

Should you include refreshments and breaks in your agenda? It depends on the length of the meeting. If the meeting will be less than an hour, a break is not usually needed. However, if the meeting is longer, you should schedule breaks about every hour or hour and a half. Most meetings I have attended allow 10–15 minutes for a break. You want to keep the group focused, but creativity and initiative suffer when people are tired. Sitting in a meeting can be exhausting. Below are some tips about breaks.

- Attendees will walk out and take a break if one is not scheduled. It is much less disruptive to have breaks rather than have people miss things while they take an individual break.

- Sometimes you only need to give participants a chance to stand and stretch.

- Food can be served during the meeting, or you can offer food during breaks. What works best for your group?

CASE STUDY

When I was administrative assistant to one of the company's highest ranking managers, I had to set up his meetings. That meant obtain the meeting room, notify all expected attendees, prepare a schedule of events and talking points and gather all pertinent material needed for the meeting including pens and paper. For luncheon meetings, I had to order the luncheons, generally sandwiches from the company cafeteria, including coffee or tea. At all evening meetings, the cafeteria would prepare the meals, much as a catering service would. (Sometimes these meetings lasted long into the evening hours, and arrangements had to be made for the janitorial crew to be kept late to clean-up. (Union Rules.) The schedule and talking points were always set at the table where each attendee would be sitting. Full pitchers of water and glasses were placed strategically on the table.

- When the meetings were classified, all security measures had to be attended to beforehand such as securing the meeting rooms. No phones, radios, computers, recorders, or listening devices were allowed, and all attendees had to be checked for their security clearance. If the security clearances were not high enough to attend the meetings called, the person was not allowed into the room. The only television allowed in the room was closed circuit.

- A large meeting room had to be reserved to accommodate attendees comfortably so that no one had to stand.

- The schedule of events had to be cleared beforehand with all talking points that the executive wished to address. All pertinent company proprietary and classified material needed for the meeting as scheduled had to be kept under lock and key until the meeting actually started.

- Notices were sent out to all those expected to attend with a definite RSVP as to why they could not attend a command meeting.

- All attendees had to be dressed appropriately at these meetings and be prepared to answer questions and formulate new ideas.

- If the conference was a luncheon, sufficient food had to be brought in for all attendees including coffee, tea, or soft drinks. No liquor was allowed at these meetings. Anyone attending these meetings who smelled of strong drink was ushered out immediately and reprimanded severely.

- Attendees had to be on time. The meetings started promptly at the time appointed and the doors were closed at that given time. Once those doors were closed, no one could enter. Those who arrived late had to wait until the meeting doors were opened for a 15-minute break to be able to enter. To say that being late for one of these meetings was frowned upon is an understatement. Those who did so would have to get the information they missed from other attendees after the meeting was over.

- When the meeting was over, all the company's proprietary and classified materials had to be secured. All paper left behind had to be picked up and destroyed before the clean-up crew was allowed in the room. (For this purpose we had what was known as burn bags where all classified and propriety material destined for destruction was placed.) These bags were taken out by a security detail and burned.

Elena Bowman
Retired Executive Secretary to a Defense Industry Consultant
http://elenadb.home.comcast.net

- It is good to have water pitchers and glasses on the tables at all times. It is simple, cheap, and will make a difference for the attendees.

Do NOT give attendees too much food or they will doze off.

Build Your Kit

If you are in meetings frequently, you can save a lot of time by creating a kit that you take to all meetings. Below is a list of items your kits can include. Are there other things you would add to this list?

- Extension cords

- Electrical outlet adapter and computer adapters if needed

- Markers to use on white board or flip chart

- Note pads, pencils, pens, and highlighters for everyone. Restock on a regular basis because you will not get all of them back at the end of the meeting.

- Disposable name tags.

- If you use an overhead projector it is always good to carry blank transparencies. You never know when it would be convenient to make notes to use on the overhead projector.

- Any time I am going to any sort of event, I like to carry duct tape, masking tape, scotch tape, push pins, thumb tacks, scissors, a short thin rope or string, clothespins, a watch or timer of some kind, and a stapler and staples. You never know when you will need one of these things.

Just before your meeting starts, take a look around the room for any possible distractions such as something blocking the attendees' view of the speaker. It can be a beautiful scene out the window, activity outside the room, unnecessary or excessive noise, light, activity, in nearby rooms. These are things that you might not think about, but they will make a difference in the success of your meetings. Following are some tips to rescue your meeting planning.

- Compile an agenda that is prioritized.
- Make it everyone's responsibility to create an effective meeting.
- Establish definite ground rules.
- Carefully plan and execute the logistics for your meeting.

Roles of Meeting Attendees

Each person involved in the meeting needs to prepare elements of the meeting. Below are examples for each type of participant. How can you use these suggestions to improve your preparation and the preparation of your participants?

Leader

The leader needs to evaluate the advisability of having a meeting. Is it necessary? If not, what are other alternatives to get the information to the appropriate people? Next, the leader needs to determine the best people to include for an effective meeting. How much participation do you need to reach goals? Your answer will affect whom you invite and how many people need to attend. Choose a facilitator and recorder. These people need to be effective. Talk to everyone who will participate in advance to be sure they are prepared. This includes having all materials, displays, and other tools needed to be ready in advance. After the materials are prepared, they need to be distributed to the appropriate people in advance.

Facilitator

The meeting facilitator should develop the agenda and establish ground rules before the meeting begins. Before the meeting, logistic information needs to be planned and any potential problems should be worked out. Some of the logistical items include when and where to have the meeting, what layout is best, whether you need refreshments, what to serve, and any materials and equipment needed. You may need a meeting planner to help coordinate large or overly complex gatherings. It is the facilitator's responsibility to create the best scenario to have the most effective meeting possible.

Participants

Many meeting participants feel they can simply show up and sit in a chair. However, participants need to participate; otherwise, they should stay at their desks and do their work. Your attendees need to understand they are being invited to the meeting for a reason. Do they understand the reason they are included and what is required of them? When you send an invitation, include details about what will be covered, the agenda, and anything in particular that you need from the participant. If there is any relevant information, participants need to review it before arriving at the meeting. Participants can also pass along suggestions about the agenda.

Specially Invited Guests

Sometimes your meeting will need experts or resource people who can bring additional information to the discussion. They need to understand what you are trying to accomplish and their part in the meeting before it starts. Any research and preparation needs to be done before the meeting. If they are doing a presentation, it needs to be ready for the meeting, and they should supply any handouts or other tools for the participants. Will they need any special equipment? This is something the facilitator or leader needs to know in advance.

In the following chapter we will discuss the steps needed to plan an effective agenda. The agenda is the plan for your meeting and it will keep you on track and help attendees understand how to prepare for the meetings. Then in Chapter 6, we will discuss some additional planning strategies to make your meetings more effective. I cannot overemphasize the importance of planning your meeting thoroughly and in advance. That is one reason why the information is broken into several chapters.

5

PLANNING YOUR MEETING AGENDA

After the agenda is complete, it should be distributed to all participants to allow them to prepare for the meeting and make suggestions about the agenda before the meeting.

There is no need to make the agenda an elaborate document. The idea is to get the information in one place and to make it readable and easy to understand. You may opt for it to be handwritten or put it on a chalkboard or poster. When the agenda is short, it can also be communicated verbally.

When you compile the agenda, keep these things in mind:

- What do you need so that the meeting stays on track?

- What do the participants need to know to prepare and participate?

- Have you listed all agenda items fully and in the proper order?

- Is the meeting time frame listed on the agenda?

- Are any breaks listed?

- Have you listed time frames for each portion of the meeting?

As the leader of the meeting, you need more detail on your copy of the agenda, but be sure to supply enough information for the participants to understand what will be discussed. The leader's agenda should include any special techniques you plan to use, any equipment or handouts that you need, and specific points that will need additional clarification.

The agenda should be sent to people who will attend and possibly your supervisor. Anyone who will be playing a more involved role in the meeting may need a more detailed agenda, such as the one you are using.

Even if the meeting is a regularly scheduled staff meeting, it is good to send out an agenda. This will inform the employees that there is a purpose for the meeting. This will make it more likely they will attend and be prepared.

This is a brief example of an agenda:

- Give the opening statement that explains the reason for the meeting, the goal, and how long it will take.
- Introduce problems to be discussed.
- Participants will discuss potential solutions to these problems.
- Evaluate and choose a solution.
- Create a plan to solve a problem.
- Assign participants tasks to work toward the chosen solution.
- Determine how the group will follow-up on the progress being made.
- Sum up the information generated and adjourn the meeting.

Now that you have a general idea of what an agenda contains, let us discuss the procedure in more detail.

CREATE A GREAT MEETING

These are the basic elements that you build upon to create a great meeting. We will discuss the opening in more detail in Chapter 7, but these are the basic things you need to do at the beginning of your meeting.

Keep in mind that your agenda will work better if you only tackle a small number of problems at your meeting. If you try to focus on too many things, you will not accomplish much. Attendees will be distracted by too many topics.

- **State Your purpose, goals, and the agenda** – This is the perfect time to be sure that the participants and attendees understand why you are having the meeting and why they were invited.

- **Establish the ground rules** – Ground Rules are covered in full detail in Chapter 4.

- **Determine the roles for participants and explain their responsibilities** – Roles of meeting attendees are discussed in Chapter 10. Understand individual roles and how certain duties work into the agenda. Will other people handle some duties? If so, which duties and how will you weave them into the meeting? Have you explained the responsibilities to each person?

- **Choose the method for making decisions** – Since a group can use a variety of ways to make decisions, Be sure to explain how the decisions will be made. The participants need to understand the procedures to be used. Some of these include

  o Voting to find a majority

  o Voting that needs a ⅔, ¾, or higher plurality to reach decision

  o Referring information and decision to a portion of the group

  o Reaching a consensus with additional considerations

  o Reaching a consensus without additional considerations

- **Additional ideas** – Any group of people is likely to come up with ideas that are good, but not for the current project. When this happens, have a procedure to write them down and to review them later, helping you to save the idea while still working to keep the meeting on track. You can schedule a time near the end of the meeting to discuss these items and possibly decide which things to add to future agendas. If it is something simple and you have time, you can address the idea at that time.

- **The next step** – It is good to have a list or chart that shows what should be done next and who will take this action.

- **Set the tone** – The facilitator needs to set the correct tone from the beginning. Being friendly and cheerful can be a great start. Acknowledge people when they enter and be helpful.

- **Introduction** – It might be good to offer a brief overview of the group and the reason it was formed along with some of its accomplishments. This is especially helpful when you have visitors.

- **Build your team** – Some groups need to work on becoming a team. If your group is not cohesive, plan some teambuilding exercises.

- **Tasks or Projects** – Usually, the main reason for having a meeting is to make a decision, find a solution, or to accomplish some other task. This objective needs to be addressed clearly.

- **Closing** – The meeting needs a decisive ending. I've attended too many meetings where the leader just sat down or people stood and left. That was the only signal that the meeting was over. These are several ways to conclude a meeting. We will discuss all these phases in more detail in Chapters 14 and 15. Which of these ideas are right for your group?

  o Review any decisions.

  o Clearly state the next steps to be taken.

  o Review additional ideas that were mentioned.

  o Evaluate the meeting along with suggested ways to improve.

  o Find a personal way to close the meeting.

At some meetings that I led, I ended with an appropriate or encouraging quote and told everyone I would see them the following week. They came to understand that when I read the quote for the day, the meeting was almost over. It was a simple procedure, but made it clear when the meeting was over.

DEVELOP YOUR AGENDA

A meeting without an agenda can be chaos. If you are the meeting leader and you decide not to use an agenda, these are some things that can happen:

- You will look unprepared and unprofessional. Strong-minded attendees may even walk out.

- Your group will be disorganized and will not accomplish as much as they should.

- Your group may end up discussing the same thing at numerous meetings because you never seem to accomplish anything.

- You may have an unusually high number of emergency meetings to handle things that were handled improperly or that were overlooked at other meetings.

It may not be obvious to you, but this sort of behavior is basically telling your employees that you are not concerned if they are unproductive. They can also get the opinion that you are not concerned with doing things in a way that provides better customer service. Wasting time and money is bad enough, but when your disorganization or lack of preparation affects customer service, you need to re-evaluate your procedures.

It is best to use active verbs when you talk to attendees. Here are some words that you should use.

Active Verbs to Spur Activity in Your Meeting			
Add	Agree	Assign	Audit
Brainstorm	Build	Calculate	Check
Classify	Combine	Compile	Complete
Compute	Conduct	Confirm	Continue
Debate	Decide	Delegate	Delete
Deliver	Determine	Divide	Draft
Edit	Evaluate	Explain	Find
Force	Gather	Give	Hear
Illustrate	Judge	Jump Start	List
Listen	Make	Map	Negotiate
Organize	Persuade	Plan	Prepare

Active Verbs to Spur Activity in Your Meeting			
Present	Preview	Rank	Rate
Read	Recommend	Report	Resolve
Rewrite	Revise	Schedule	Select
Set Up	Share	Simplify	Sketch
Solution	Solve	Suggest	Summarize
Tell	Trace	Visit	Write

Using this list will also help you to word things in a positive and motivating way.

While you are thinking the list above, beware of overused words These are "key words" that people tend to use too often and your attendees may tune you out when you use these words. Those words include:

- Administer
- Analyze
- Assure
- Collaborate
- Coordinate
- Develop
- Ensure
- Establish

- Examine
- Expedite
- Follow-up
- Implement
- Investigate
- Manage
- Observe
- Perform

PUT IT TOGETHER

We've discussed previously that the agenda needs to be prepared in advance and then distributed to the proposed attendees. It must be done at least one day before the meeting, but it would be much better if it was ready one week ahead.

One issue with creating an agenda is the time involved. I would suggest creating a form to use for planning your agenda. Following is an example.

<u>Agenda</u>

Group Name _____ Date _____

Meeting Title _____ Start Time _____

Meeting Organizer _____ Ending Time _____

Location_____

Type of Meeting (Check one): Speaker ☐ Presentation ☐ Planning ☐
Problem Solving ☐ Other ☐

Materials Needed for Meeting _____

_____

What Should Participants Bring _____

_____

Goals for the Meeting _____

_____

Meeting Leader _____ Recorder _____

Facilitator _____ Decision Maker _____

Group Members to be Included _____

_____

_____

_____

Special Notes for Attendees or Leader_____

_____

Visitors_____

These are the individual elements of the Agenda Planning Form.

Group Name – Does your group have a name? If not, it can be good to have a name. This will identify the specific group of people and can create a team atmosphere.

Date – What is the date for the meeting? It is good to include date and day of the week.

Meeting Title – Is it a monthly or weekly sales meeting? It could be a special planning meeting or maybe a special problem solving meeting. Give your meeting a title.

Start Time – Indicate starting time and then begin on time.

Meeting Organizer – Who called the meeting? Include the name so that people can contact then with questions or suggestions.

Ending Time – Indicate the ending time and make an effort to end on time.

Location – Where will the meeting be held? Include enough detail so that everyone can find the meeting. If it is off site, include any necessary directions and transportation information if needed.

Type of Meeting – (Speaker, Presentation, Problem Solving, Planning, or Other) Choose one of these types of meetings or indicate if it is something different to help attendees understand how they need to prepare.

Materials Needed for Meeting –Include any materials you will distribute to participants. Give them a checklist to be sure they have everything they need for the meeting.

What Should Participants Bring - List any materials that participants need to bring. It is also good to make a note about who is participating and who is merely attending.

Goals for the Meeting – List your specific goals for the meeting. What do you need to accomplish? Make this clear before the meeting starts.

Meeting Leader – Who will lead the meeting?

Recorder – Who is responsible to record details and minutes from the meeting?

Facilitator – Who will facilitate the meeting?

Decision Maker – Who are the decision makers who set the goals for your meeting?

Group Members to be Included – List all members who are to attend.

Special Notes for Attendees or Leader – Do you have special information that the participants need to know? If so, list the information here.

Visitors – List any visitors that you expect to attend, including people from outside the business or usual attendees.

Outline Each Item

Another way to examine what needs to be included on your agenda is to fill out a simple form for each item. You could have an individual sheet of paper for each item or include several on one page. This is a sample that you can use or adjust to fit your needs.

Possible Agenda Item

Our team needs to –

_____

This is why this item came to my attention –

_____

These are the benefits of dealing with the problem –

_____

It should take _____ minutes to discuss this issue and to find a solution.

Compile a list of the elements of the agenda that others will handle. There needs to be a firm decision on how they will handle their portion, how to move from the main portion of the meeting to their work, any materials or equipment they need, and whether they need to prepare their own agenda for their segment.

Below are some tips to help you make an effective and complete agenda:

- Make a list of all possible topics to be covered.

- What process will be used and how much time is needed for each element of the meeting?

- Add the estimated time for each section of the meeting to determine if your potential topics need to be cut back or expanded. (It is rare that you need to expand an agenda.)

- It is common to have too many topics requiring too much time.

- Cut down your agenda and make it manageable within a realistic time frame.

- A manageable agenda will make your meeting a success.

- Decide whether to start with the more complicated topics or whether to start with the easier topics. There are advantages and disadvantages of both. Make the decision on which practice is better for your group and you might make adjustments to this process over time.

- A normal order for meetings is: Reports, Urgent Topics, and Common Topics

- With this normal order it ensures the most important things are covered even if you run out of time.

All meeting leaders and facilitators need to be careful not to be bogged down with "putting out fires," a waste of time. Better organization will help you stay focused on the topics that need to be handled. You can call a periodic meeting for the purpose of handling emergency items. At these meetings everyday issues should not be considered.

You may consider labeling your agenda as a "suggested" agenda. This will encourage the participants to offer their suggestions and will help them be more involved in the meeting preparation. You can set aside a bit of time to review the items with participants. All these steps get attendees involved and give them a stake in making the meeting a success.

SAVE TIME IN YOUR MEETING

The more active your meeting is, the more time it will take. This is another reason to plan the agenda thoroughly. Earlier we discussed the cost of having a meeting, so it is advisable not to waste any time. These are some tips to help you save time.

- **Start Time** – This sounds like a no-brainer, but many meetings start late. Include a recommended arrival time and the start time on your agenda. This will also help tardy people understand that they need to be there on time. They need to arrive on time.

- **Be Clear** – Make the instructions clear and, if necessary, commit them to paper. Include instructions on the agenda that is distributed to head off opening distractions.

- **Material Distribution** – Circulate the materials ahead of time. Be sure you get the materials out to attendees in plenty of time for them to prepare.

- **Visual Aids** – These materials also need to be created and distributed ahead of time. Make sure they are transported to the meeting location.

- **Reports** – If you conduct a meeting using subgroups to find possible solutions, have the subgroups report their findings on a display board for easy review. Another solution is to have each group pick their favorite suggestion and only report on that item.

- **Pick up the Pace** – Do not let the discussion grow stagnant. Keep things moving and keep the participants moving through the topics or problems.

- **Draft the Help You Need** – If you need volunteers, pick them out of the crowd. This will save dead time by waiting for people to volunteer.

- **Prepare for Sluggishness** – Have a list of questions or possible topics prepared to get the creative juices flowing for tired groups.

- **Keep Moving** – There are times when you need to nudge the group to keep moving.

- **Additional Ideas** – When the group has additional comments that are good but do not apply to the current topic, have someone assigned to list them. If you stop to consider tangential items, you will lose time. Discuss them later.

STEPS FOR AN EFFECTIVE MEETING

The meeting leader and participants have various things they need to do to make the meeting effective. There are things that should be done before, during, and after the meeting. Below I have listed these responsibilities for the leader and participants.

Meeting Leader

Before

- State and understand the purpose of the meeting
- Decide which people need to attend and why they need to be there
- Contact potential attendees to ensure they can attend
- Schedule a room for the meeting
- Schedule or reserve any equipment that is needed
- Arrange for the necessary refreshments
- Prepare the agenda
- Distribute agenda along with invitation to all proposed attendees
- Check the room before the meeting to ensure things are ready

During

- Start the meeting on time
- Stick to your agenda
- Manage your time

- Control the amount of discussion and stop any unrelated chit chat

- Encourage attendees to participate

- Be aware of conflicts and problems and help resolve these

- Make it clear to the attendees what action is needed

- Sum up the high points of the meeting and reiterate what needs to be done

After

- Rearrange the room and remove all of your equipment and materials

- Honestly evaluate the meeting's effectiveness

- Forward evaluation forms to meeting attendees to gather their feedback

- Circulate memo about any discussion from the meeting

- Move forward with the action that is needed

- Proceed with action that is needed and was decided upon

The participants also have responsibilities before, during, and after the meeting. This is a list of their responsibilities.

Participants

Before

- Schedule time for the meeting

- Confirm that you will be in attendance

- Be sure that you understand what is required of you

- You may be able to suggest additional people who need to be in attendance or who can contribute valuable information to the proposed agenda items

- Understand the goals and purpose of the meeting

- Be clear on when and where to meet

- Do any advance preparation to be prepared for the meeting

During

- Listen to the leader and speaker

- Participate when required

- Open your mind and actually listen

- Avoid any distractions and unrelated conversations

- If you have questions, ask them and be sure you understand

- Take notes, especially about action steps that need to be taken

After

- Personally evaluate the effectiveness of the meeting

- Review the information in the memo and ask questions if something appears wrong or confusing

- Discuss with people who need to know the details

- Move forward with the action that was discussed and agreed upon. Proceed with the necessary action.

When you have attendees who do not participate or contribute anything to the meeting, you might want to share this list with them. It never hurts to make sure your attendees understand they have responsibilities in your meetings. They are not there to take up space and eat; they need to participate.

Now that you understand the duties for the leader and also the attendees and you have an agenda in place, let us focus on where to meet and how to arrange the room for the most effective meeting.

6

STRATEGIC MEETING PLANNING

———

Many people figure they can meet anywhere without giving it significant thought and preparation. You can, but doing so will lower the effectiveness of your meeting. When we are in a good location with a good setup, we do not notice. A bad location and the wrong setup is noticeable. The wrong setting will distract attendees from the information you are presenting.

Does your business have meeting rooms available? That can be a great advantage, but do not assume that is your best option. We will discuss qualities of an ideal location for your meeting and working with another facility to prepare your meeting room.

CHOOSE THE RIGHT ROOM

The first thing to do is to determine the minimum and maximum number of people who will attend your meeting. Once you have this number, you need to find a room to fit that number of people. It needs to be big enough for your attendees, table and chair setup, and any equipment and visual aids you plan to use. There may be times when the number of attendees changes substantially so that you may need change the room and layout.

It is not always possible to get the exact room that you want. For this reason, it is good to have several choices listed in the order of your top preference. It is difficult to visualize how many people will fit in a room. Find people who used the rooms before and ask them about the layout and attendance that they had in the room. This can be valuable and helpful until you get used to setting up meeting rooms.

Do not be overly concerned about the shape of potential meeting rooms, because most rooms will be square or rectangular. If you are considering a room that is an unusual shape, be sure that it will provide space for the set-up that you need.

OPTIONS TO ARRANGE YOUR ROOM

There are many possible room arrangements. We will discuss which arrangements are beneficial for different sorts of meetings. You may find that you have more than one option. In this case, look at the room and consider your group to see which one would be better for your people.

Here are some of the things that you should consider to create the ideal situation for your meeting room.

- **Access** – Before the meeting, determine whether it is easy to get into the room? Are bathrooms located nearby? It is also good to check the fire escape.

- **Cooling, Heating, and Ventilation** – The temperature in the room makes a big difference. When it is too cool or too warm people are distracted. Sufficient ventilation is also important for your attendees. If the room is cold, hot, or the air is stale, talk to someone about fixing this problem. This is a good reason to check the room in person before your meeting instead of just making a phone call. Make sure the room has a thermostat that is accessible to you.

- **Furnishings and Equipment** – It is important to have sufficient, comfortable seating—especially for longer meetings. Have puzzles and games for brainstorming sessions because they can create an open-minded atmosphere for the meeting. For some occasions you might eliminate the tables and even the chairs. Stand-up meetings can get ideas flowing and create a sense of urgency.

- **Lights** – Your meeting room needs direct, bright light. Accessory lighting may be attractive, but it is not the best option for your meeting.

- **Location** – Is the location convenient and easy to find so attendees can get to the meeting on time? Provide a map or directions if needed.

- **Noise** – Be sure there are no loud or distracting noises. Check for any exterior noises outside or in adjoining rooms.

- **Size** – A room that fits will promote a team atmosphere and a more personal setting for discussions. Allow space for visual aids, projector screens, and flip charts. If you must use a big room, move plants and screens to block off other sections of the room.

ROOM ARRANGEMENT CHECKLIST

This checklist is for choosing a room for your meeting. Consider each item carefully before making your final decision.

Checklist for Your Meeting Room
Answer Yes or No for each question.
_____ 1. Is the room too big or too small?
_____ 2. Is there enough room for any audio visual aids that are needed?
_____ 3. Does the room have sufficient lighting, ventilation, and temperature control?
_____ 4. Can the light, vent, and temperature be controlled in the room?
_____ 5. Are there any loud noises or foul odors around the room?

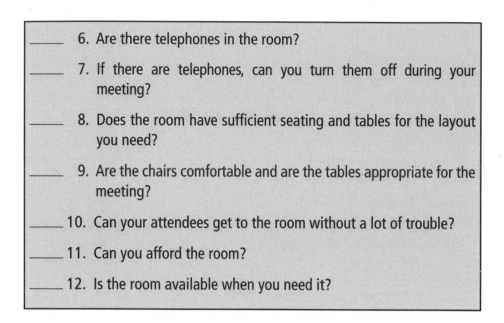

_____ 6. Are there telephones in the room?

_____ 7. If there are telephones, can you turn them off during your meeting?

_____ 8. Does the room have sufficient seating and tables for the layout you need?

_____ 9. Are the chairs comfortable and are the tables appropriate for the meeting?

_____ 10. Can your attendees get to the room without a lot of trouble?

_____ 11. Can you afford the room?

_____ 12. Is the room available when you need it?

ARRANGEMENT TYPES

The seating and table arrangement you choose make a big difference in the dynamics of your meeting. I have included a number of different options and illustrations of each type.

Circular seating options are best for discussion meetings. A closed circle creates a more intimate feeling and encourages a team atmosphere. It intensifies the mood of the group, whether good or bad. If attendees show up and the mood is negative or ugly, shift a few chairs to create a semi circle. This does not require much effort, but can help calm the mood of your group.

There are a number of room layout options. The type of layout depends on the size of the room, the number of attendees, the way the meeting will be conducted, and what you need to accomplish. Take a look at the diagrams and the descriptions to decide which layout is best for each meeting.

Remember that discussions are more coherent if participants can see each other. For these meetings, it is good to use circles, squares, semi circles, or U-shape arrangements.

Circles and Squares

The advantage of this layout encourages all attendees to participate and interact with each other, but it requires you to decide whether to use tables. They are convenient if your participants need to make notes, but they can inhibit communication. That does not mean you cannot use tables; just be sure they are needed. This layout also shifts the focus away from the leader and onto all participants equally.

Circles and squares can be difficult with more than 15 people. Will you need a screen, flip chart, or other visual aids? If so, you need to find a way to display these items for all attendees to see. That can be complicated with this arrangement. Circles are ideal for communication, but squares are not as effective. Squares will work although there may be less discussion. Oval and rectangular layouts are similar to circular and square arrangements. Use circles for meeting with up to 12 to 15 attendees.

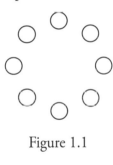

Figure 1.1

2–8 people

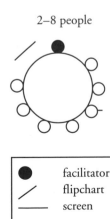

Figure 1.2

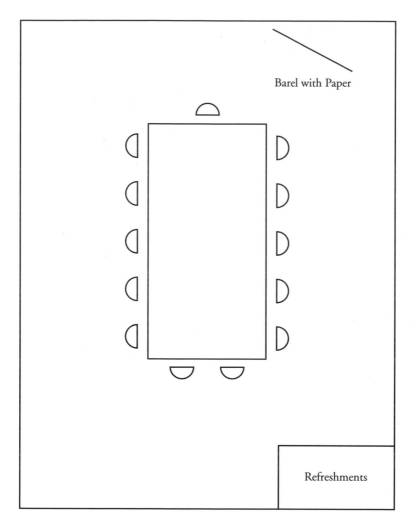

Barel with Paper

Refreshments

Figure 1.3

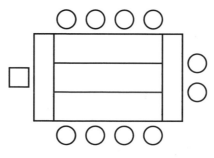

Figure 1.4

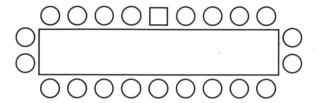

Figure 1.5

If the group is larger, you can create multiple circles within the larger group to allow for sub groups. This is ideal for problem-solving, discussion, and brainstorming sessions. An oval setup can make it difficult to see the people beside you.

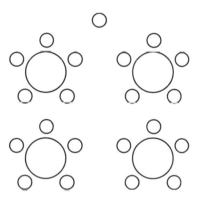

Figure 1.6

30–200 people

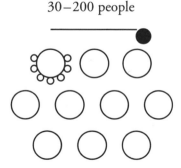

Figure 1.7

Another variation would be the placement of eight tables with two chairs at each table. This allows all attendees to see each other and to create a team atmosphere between the people seated together.

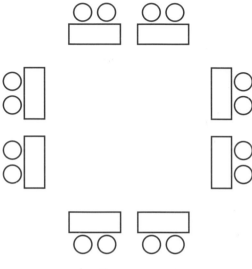

Figure 1.8

Semi Circles and U-Shaped Layouts

These layouts are good for problem-solving, discussions, and meetings with attendee participation. Semi-circles and U-shape room layouts are good for meetings with visual aids. The meeting leader and visual aids can be placed at the "open" end of the room. It is natural for attendees to look to the "front" of the setup. A circle layout is more intense, but many times a semi-circle or U-shape is the most effective choice. On the other hand this setup is not conducive for a large group. These are not the best layout for a small area because there is wasted room. Another benefit to the U-shape is that the meeting leader can easily approach each attendee to talk, show them something, pass out handouts and many other things.

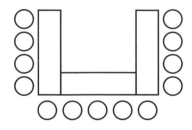

Figure 2.1

Semi-circles should be oriented to a wall where you can display visual aids. People will tend to look at the door each time it opens. With regular meetings in one particular room, you can stop people from arriving late or leaving early by facing the attendees toward the door. This will mean they are noticed by everyone when they arrive or leave and will be put on the spot.

If you have more than 15 attendees, the "U" can look like a bowling alley and it can detract from potential benefits. You may seat some people within the "U." It is not as convenient for discussion, but will help you keep attendees facing the front and create more seating in a smaller space. You can also use the U-shape with satellite tables at each corner. See Figure 2.3.

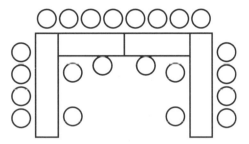

Figure 2.2

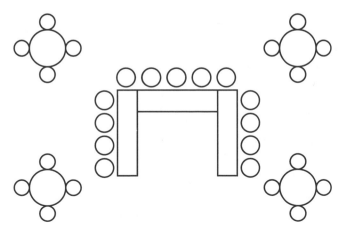

Figure 2.3

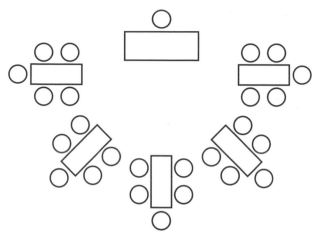

Figure 2.4

This can be adjusted to use tables in a semi-circle with multiple people sitting at each table, allowing attendees to focus on the meeting leader while participants at individual tables work together. This style is great for problem solving when you want small groups to work together.

Theatre Style Seating

In a meeting with many attendees, theatre style is ideal for arranging seats in parallel rows, either in line with the front or diagonal to maximize the space you have available. Keep in mind that theatre seating is not conducive to discussions and interaction between the attendees. If you must use a large auditorium area but there are few attendees, have them sit in the center or in one section to create a team atmosphere.

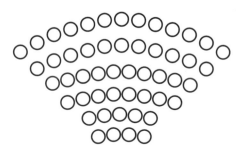

Figure 3.1

Parallel or diagonal can depend on the space available and the best way for all attendees to have a good view of the front of the room. When the seats are angled, the attendees can see some of the other people. Rows that are parallel to the front of the room will only allow attendees to see the back of people's heads.

Classroom Seating

This style is good for training meetings. It keeps your attendees facing forward and gives them a place to write or place materials on the table in front of them. It is better if you can angle the tables, but sometimes that is not possible. This is not your best layout for meetings where you need participation. You can use individual tables with three or four attendees at each to encourage them to work together as a group.

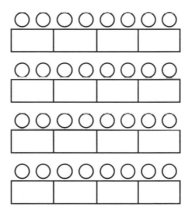

Figure 3.2a

You can arrange the seating with or without tables depending on the room you have and whether tables are actually needed. All eyes are generally focused on the speaker or meeting leader. This arrangement can maximize the space you have and will allow attendees to make notes and review handouts.

This arrangement will allow you to get more people into a smaller space instead of circles or squares, and attendees have a place to make notes. However, it can be a negative reminder of school and participation is reduced because people cannot see each other.

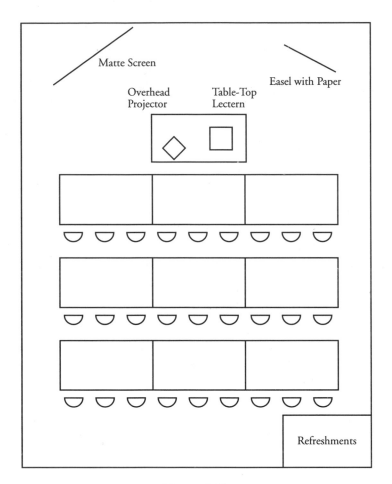

Figure 3.2b

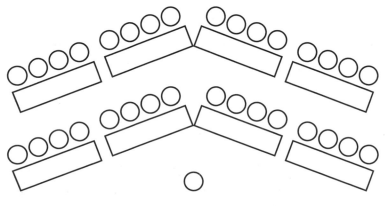

Figure 3.3a

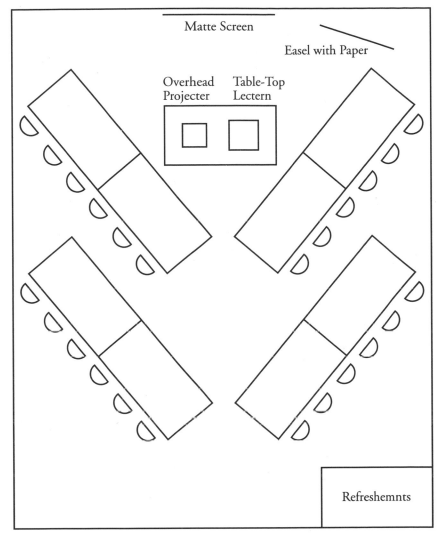

Figure 3.3b

Seating Rules of Thumb

Here are some specific things to remember when arranging the seating for your meeting.

- If you use square tables, only place one person on the end to give everyone enough room.

- You can sit 10–12 people around a 72" round table. A 60" table is more common, and it will seat 10 if necessary.

- Each attendee needs about two feet of room including their seat and room beside them. However, three feet is much better especially if they will be taking notes. Six-foot tables are common and you can fit two or three people at each table.

Layout Checklists

This is one checklist to help you double-check the arrangement.

Checklist — Meeting Arrangements
_____ 1. Table and chairs properly arranged.
_____ 2. Place name cards on table. (Do not need if everyone is acquainted.)
_____ 3. Chalkboard, white board, or flip chart is ready, if needed.
_____ 4. Overhead projector is ready and in working order.
_____ 5. Other equipment is ready and in working order.
_____ 6. Appropriate refreshments are ready and available.
_____ 7. Breaks have been scheduled at appropriate intervals.
_____ 8. Have a smoking policy in place. Best to have no smoking if possible.
_____ 9. You have all handouts, paper, sharpened pencils, and other materials ready.

PREPARING THE SPACE

It is critical to prepare the meeting space before the meeting begins. The appearance of the room makes a difference, especially if you have visitors. Consider outside noises: I scheduled a meeting once in a local restaurant. The room was big enough for our group and the restaurant was willing to let us in before they opened for our meeting. The meeting was a little cramped, but it was going well until about 9:30 a.m. There was a loud noise from outside. They neglected to mention that the dumpster, would be emptied that morning. The noise totally distracted everyone. I never would have thought to ask about a dumpster schedule, but I think about it now.

Check these elements of the facility.

- **Lighting** – Is it sufficient?

- **Cleanliness** – Has the room been cleaned including the chairs, tables, and floor?

- **Audiovisual Equipment** – Do a test to be sure the equipment is working.

- **Flip Charts and Chalkboards** – Provide sufficient places for notes and visual aids.

- **Temperature** – Keep it cool enough in the summer and not too warm in the winter.

- **Air and Ventilation** – Is there enough ventilation? If you will be using the air conditioning or heat for the first time that season, it is good to make sure it works and has no odor.

- **Noise** – Are there distracting noises of any kind? If so, find a way to stop them.

- **Music** – Some soft background noise might be good during breaks or when the group breaks into smaller groups. Be sure that you have control over the volume.

- **Furniture** – Do you have the chairs and tables you need? Be sure you have enough and that it is not broken or defective in any way.

- **Size and Arrangement** – Make sure the room is big enough. A room that is too big can be distracting to your attendees. Also, be sure the room is set up properly to accomplish your objectives.

Projector Screens

The size of projector screens makes a big difference to the attendees. Below are the common standards to consider. The size of the screen is determined by the distance from the attendees to the screen.

Distance to the Screen	20'	25'	30'	35'	40'
Screen Size	50" x 50"	60" x 60"	70" x 70"	84" x 84"	96" x 96"

These are some tips for better projector placement.

- Place screen so that it can be viewed from all seats.

- Be sure speaker or projector are not in the way.

- If the speaker is right handed, place screen to his right. If the speaker is left handed, place the screen to his left.

- A screen with a matte finish gives a better picture when viewed from an angle.

- Place the speaker on one side of the narrow end of the room.

- Use the distance from the screen to the person seated furthest away from it.

- Tilt the screen forward at the top to eliminate distortion.

Create a Friendly Setting

Your meeting attendees need to be comfortable. They should not be too comfortable and especially in the afternoon, because they may go to sleep. For meetings longer than an hour, it is best to offer chairs with cushions. The nature of your meeting will dictate whether you need tables or desks. For events that include speeches or presentations, your attendees should need only a chair. This will save space and make set easier. Room temperature is important. It should not be too warm or too cold. Sixty eight degrees is an ideal temperature.

When you arrange a meeting room, you want to create a friendly setting and atmosphere. These are some tips to help you.

- Can participants see each other?

- Will you supply something to write with and something to write on? If so, will they have tables?

- Are participants free to use chalkboards or flip charts to give more details?

- Do you allow participants to move around to relieve tension, usually during a longer meeting?

- Will you supply food and drink for meetings that last more than two hours?

Inspect all equipment, materials, food, seats, and tables before the meeting begins. It is also advisable to be sure all equipment is working and all materials are complete and ready for use. A missing extension cords, a wrong electrical outlet, blown lamp bulbs, and similar things seem small, but they will grind your meeting to a halt.

BODY LANGUAGE OF YOUR ATTENDEES

Consult books and articles about how to interpret body language. It is a form of nonverbal communication that convey meaning to others. Body language includes:

- Facial expressions

- Movements

- Sitting position

- Crossed arms or legs

- Stance

- Posture

Body language reveals more than your words. The tip-offs to your feelings are in how your arms are crossed, the way you cross your legs, the way you hold your mouth, how your brow is furrowed, whether you slouch in your seat, tension that is obvious on your face, direct or indirect eye contact, leaning forward, or leaning back in your chair.

When you learn to read these nonverbal signals, it is possible to understand more about your meeting attendees, but be aware that they can also read your body language. What are your body and your movements saying about your mood or attitude? Is it conveying the right message to your attendees?

The group members' body language communicates how they feel about each other. Do they stand close and lean toward each other? Or do they stand far apart and seem to avoid each other? All of these postures tell you details about your group. Watch their interaction to find the problem people and problem areas.

It is common in a group for some people to stay close to each other, while others make an effort to avoid each other. A simple way to shake this up is to assign seats and rearrange the usual seating arrangement. You may need to enforce the new seating plan. Another way is to assign different people to work together. Find people who can complement each other's skills and knowledge, but who might not be social with each other. They may work together well although they would not find their way to each other.

The seat you choose can make a difference in where the attendees sit. Could you sit in the middle of a group that alienate themselves? What about asking certain people to sit near you? It is possible to make meeting assignments and have them sit near you. These techniques can be subtle and effective. All of these things will help you build a team instead of a bunch of individual groups at odds with each other.

Do you have certain people who disrupt your meetings? Make every effort to split up these groups of people or only invite specific members of the group. They may choose to sit in a position that gives them power. Have them sit up front or somewhere close to you. This makes it easier to keep an eye on them and to react quickly to their shenanigans. When a disruptive person sits in the back, the other attendees turn their attention away from the speaker or leader when the person talks. The disrupters need to sit in a different section of the room.

Are there empty seats in your meeting room? It is best to have the attendees move closer together. This may sound funny, but an occasional empty chair can zap the energy from your group. When they sit side by side, the group works better together.

PROVIDE FOOD IF NEEDED

You will not need food for every meeting, but there are times when it is advisable to offer refreshments. Avoid full meals because of the time and expense involved. Meals also offer far too many variations and can be complicated. Here are tips about what sort of breaks and refreshments are recommended.

CASE STUDY

We planned a long day meeting for Valley Community Services Board to plan how to implement long-term training.

Meeting location – Monterey, VA - Church Recreation Area

Visitor – Speaker to do Training

Break – Lunch at the Highland Inn, a short walk from the meeting location

We walked to the Highland Inn for lunch—a great time for us to eat and discuss the points that were presented in training. The break also helped us prepare mentally and physically for the afternoon session on how to set goals to apply the information we learned.

Richard Henkel, Former Board Member and Treasurer
Valley Community Service Board, Staunton, VA

Breaks – A 15-minute break is recommended for 90 minutes of meeting time to allow attendees to go to the restroom, get a drink and snack, and make a phone call.

Breakfast – A continental breakfast can be great for a morning meeting. Some meetings allow for attendees to arrive early to eat, while others offer food and drink during the meeting. That decision is up to the meeting leader based on the group's preferences.

Lunch – A simple lunch can work well. The length of time should depend on the difficulty of being served in your locale.

Dinner – Recommendations are that you allow one and a half or two hours for a sit down meal. I would think a full dinner for your meeting should be a rare event. As an alternative, an evening meeting can be scheduled after the normal dinner hour.

MEETING IN ANOTHER LOCATION

At times you may need to meet off-site. Many meetings can usually be held at your office or business, but there are times when no adequate rooms are available. Sometimes the meeting is a special event that requires a larger room or special setting. You do need to be prepared for additional work for off-site meetings. Some of the locations that have room available include:

- Restaurants
- Conference Centers
- Hotels
- Libraries

Each of these facilities has a manager and may have someone in charge of their meeting rooms. You need to contact that person and see what is available. Some of the questions you need to ask are:

- What do you have available for the date I need?

- Is there more than one room?
- What amenities does each room offer?
- How many people will each room hold?
- Do you offer refreshments?
- Is there convenient parking available for my attendees?
- Is there a charge to park? If so, how much is the charge?
- Are there sufficient restrooms near the meeting room?
- What services do you offer?
- Will the facility set up the room as per my requirements?
- Do you supply enough tables, chairs, podiums, and equipment for the meeting I have planned?
- Can I ship packages of materials and visual aids to your facility?
- Can you supply me with a price list for the room and any additional services?

You may need to make some concessions. It could be helpful to determine ahead of time which items are negotiable. However, if the facility wants you to lower all your expectations, I would keep looking for another location or consider changing your meeting day and time.

It is important to visit the site personally before you commit to a contract, giving you a chance to ensure the location is right. Usually, meetings off-site are important, so double-check the facility. The next section includes a list of some of the people whose job is to help customers at a facility so that your meeting runs more smoothly. Do not be shy about asking them to help when needed.

You must remember to transport everything that you will need for an off-site meeting. Make a list and assemble everything well before the meeting; then make sure they are taken to the meeting location. Leaving behind one small item can cause problems at your meeting. It is also good have someone double-check your supplies, materials, handouts, and visual aids. This is where your "meeting kit" comes in handy, as mentioned before.

Coordinate with These People

When you meet off-site, you will need to coordinate your efforts with the venue's staff members. Here are tips to provide as much information as possible.

- *Bellboys* – They run errands, find supplies you need, and help direct attendees to your meeting.

- *Front Desk Staff* – It is also critical that they know your group is there so they can direct attendees to your meeting. I've been to meetings where the front desk staff did not have any information, and it made things difficult for attendees plus making a bad impression on visitors.

- *Kitchen Staff* – If you plan to offer refreshments, you will have contact with the kitchen. Should problems arise, do not act harshly. Notify the kitchen staff of the problem and work to find a solution.

- *Security Staff* – It is always good to be in touch with security for any event, especially in a facility that is foreign to you.

- *Shipping Department Staff* – Any materials or equipment that you need to send ahead will go through the shipping department. Be courteous and patient with these people. They can make or break your meeting.

CASE STUDY

The meetings I set up now are mostly classroom experiences. I am an instructor for UCLA Extension's Writers' Program and I also speak at other venues for writers' conferences, expos, and just about any other place writers congregate. I find it is essential to determine in advance if the sponsor will print my handouts rather than my lugging a suitcase from city to city. I also ask if the sponsor has a limit as to how many pages they will copy. I like to send my attendees off with valuable handouts and excerpts from my how-to book,. I prefer to make my own copies instead of having them inadvertently cropped or blurred by the organization's printing office. I always like to include a page of resources such as my newsletter, "Sharing with Writers," the writers' organization I founded, Authors' Coalition, and any seminars I have coming up. Promotion is part of the game!

Submitted by:
Carolyn Howard-Johnson
http://carolynhoward-johnson.com

Carolyn Howard-Johnson, Author *The Frugal Book Promoter: How to Do What Your Publisher Will Not*

Winner USA Book News' "Best Professional Book 2004" and Book Publicists of Southern California's Irwin Award.

7

EFFECTIVE WAYS TO START YOUR MEETING

You can entice or lose your audience in the opening minutes of any meeting. It is important to get their attention and show them that you are prepared. Experienced meeting attendees will know right away if you are unprepared.

The key to a great meeting is preparation. This is true no matter what type of meeting you have. Short meetings may only need a statement of the purpose and what you plan to accomplish. Longer, more detailed meetings require a complete agenda that explains the group needs, the purpose, the roles for attendees, and the logistics for the meeting.

Typical advice is to arrive at the meeting room 10 minutes early if you have things to set up, but I have never cut my entrance that close when I am leading a meeting. I like to get there 15 minutes early and set up. It usually only takes a couple of minutes, but it gives me time to talk to people as they arrive. The personal "hello" helps make us feel like a group. I've attended meetings where the leader arrived just before the meeting and did not get to speak to anyone. It did not provide the same dynamic as being able to speak together beforehand.

GETTING A GOOD START

First, start on time especially good when you meet with the same people on a regular basis. Your prompt behavior will make it clear that you expect them on time and when they learn your meetings start on time, they will be prompt and ready to start at that time.

You may distribute the agenda ahead of time, at the meeting, have a copy posted, or do all three. At the least, you can post the purpose and goal for the meeting at the front of the room to keep them in the minds of the attendees. It is important that you stay focused on this goal, or it can raise questions.

At times some people will be absent or late. In this case you may need to rearrange the schedule to accommodate these problems. You need to make a determination about how long to wait for latecomers. In some instances, the affected agenda item can be rearranged or possibly rescheduled. When you are waiting for the CEO of the company, everyone needs to wait.

If you schedule someone who is frequently late or absent, ask the person to forward his or her notes or have someone take their place, but give the substitute time to prepare. Only certain people can do this on the spur of the moment. Learn which people will help you.

There will be times when you may be unavoidably detained. In these instances, it is good to have a facilitator who can start the meeting and others on the agenda who can start their portions of the meeting until you arrive. This is another example of advance preparation helping you to handle a last minute problem.

Warm Up the Group

Even a business meeting needs some social interaction. Whether you speak with attendees before the meeting or talk with them after, you need some socialization jump starts to "warm them up" and generate a team feeling such as:

- getting everyone involved from the beginning.

- letting the attendees share their concerns or needs.

- breaking the ice for people who do not know each other.

When you have attendees who do not know each other, a productive warm up is to have each attendee share the following information.

- Name

- Department or Business

- Job Title or Position

- Time in the Business or Department

- Why They Were Asked to Attend

- What Contribution They Can Make

If there are only some new people in attendance, many meeting leaders will only ask those people to introduce themselves. This is bad because the new people do not know the established members of the group. It also makes the new attendees feel like outsiders.

What is the Tone of Your Meeting?

Starting off with a friendly and group-oriented warm up can set a great tone for the meeting. You have already asked each person to contribute something making it easier for them to participate throughout the meeting. Many times, the first comment is the hardest. It is also best to keep the tone friendly and reasonably informal.

Remember that a productive and effective meeting requires work from the leader, the facilitator, the recorder, and every other person in attendance. The people you invited are essential to making the meeting a success and they need to contribute their thoughts and suggestions. Sharing information about themselves will create a sense of community. This feeling will help each attendee feel more vested in the meeting and they will work to make it a success.

Earlier, we discussed establishing ground rules for your group. As a quick refresher, let us review the basic ground rules that your group needs. They include:

- Be prompt and ready to start on time.

- Participate in the meeting.

- Accept your assigned role and perform it to the best of your ability.

- Determine rule about cell phones and pagers.

- Show respect for each other.

- Establish discussion procedures to be used.

- Determine how confidentiality issues will be handled.

- Make assignments for attendees.

- Determine how meetings will be evaluated.

- Repercussions for frequent violation of the rules.

At first your group may need to review the rules at the beginning of each meeting. Keep an eye on the right time to dispense with reading the rules, but certain rules may need to be reviewed from time to time. The group may need to set aside time to review the rules periodically to see if changes are needed. Do not feel tied to the rules. If changes are needed, schedule time on the next agenda to discuss changes.

TECHNIQUES TO USE WITH ATTENDEES

Many leaders want to jump right into the business segment of the meeting, but sometimes that is not the best way to get things started. We've talked about the benefits of building the team atmosphere, and the remainder of this chapter will show you ways to help the attendees get to know each other and to get them to talk with each other. This promotes a team atmosphere. Easing attendees into the business element will also bring their attention into the meeting and draw them away from outside distractions. You can also explain how the meeting will be handled and reiterate what is expected from the attendees.

Call Meeting to Order

Active meetings can be busy and sometimes you may have problems calling the group to order. You need to call the meeting to order at the beginning, but you may need to do something similar after discussion periods on your agenda. After breaks is another time you will need to call the meeting to order. Here are some suggestions:

- Use a chime, bell, whistle, or any other non-offensive noise maker.

- Turn the lights off and back on to get their attention.

- Clap your hands to get their attention. (Of course, this could prompt them to clap.)

- Some groups respond to a hand signal, but that will not work with everyone.

Get the Group Moving

Sometimes it is hard to get the attendees involved in the meeting. This is especially true early in the morning or right after lunch. These are some ideas to get attendees' attention.

- **Slow Breathing** – Get the attendees to breathe slowly. It must be deep, cleansing breaths. Inhale deeply and exhale deeply.

- **Yawning Contest** – Who can yawn the loudest?

- **Movies and Books** – Give attendees one minute to call out the names of their favorite books and movies.

- **Play with Paper Airplanes** – Give everyone a piece of paper to make a paper airplane and then let everyone fly them.

- **Mirror Mirror** – Pair off attendees and have one start the movements and have the other attendee mirror their movements.

These are just a few possible ways to get people involved, moving, and thinking. Then you can dive into the meeting agenda.

GAMES TO GET YOUR MEETING STARTED

Sometimes a simple game can get things started and get the attendees to loosen up. Do not spend a lot of time playing games, but help your attendees get to know each other. There is a variety of "games" in these pages. You may choose to use one or more. Do not leave the group mood and attitude to chance. It is much better to use methods to create a positive, friendly team atmosphere.

A Bit of Humor

Why You Play – This is a creative way to bring some humor to the meeting.

How to Play – Tell the attendees this is a little light entertainment before you get to the serious part of the meeting. Break the attendees into smaller groups and give them an assignment. They might find comic ways to increase company revenues. The groups need to present the results to the whole group.

Make Some Changes – They might make an alternate agenda. You can also create a "test" based on the subjects on your agenda and add some humorous answer choices. Have them pick the answer that could not be right.

Bingo

Why You Play – This will help the attendees get to know each other.

What You Need – You need to supply "bingo" cards and pens or pencils.

MEETING BINGO				
Wearing Red	Single Parent	Has Grandchildren	Buys Lottery Tickets	Drives a Sports Car
Likes Cats	Has Red Hair	Speaks Foreign Language	Skis	Likes Dogs
Can Fly A Plane	Likes to Camp	FREE SPACE	Plays Piano	Drives a Pickup
Attended the Olympics	Plays Baseball	Has Tropical Fish	Hates Football	Hates Spinach
Visited Foreign Country	Plays Tennis	Loves Football	Has Three Children	Reads *Time* Magazine

How to Play – Let the attendees know that you will be playing bingo. The game requires them to circulate and speak to each other. Players need to fill up a horizontal, vertical, or diagonal line on the card. They do this by finding someone in the room that fits each requirement on the card. The details on the card can be personal or business related. When they find a person, have the person initial the card in one space and they have learned more about the people in the meeting.

Tips and Suggestions – The attendees can use any method to find the people they need. When you have fewer attendees, it may be better to make the board smaller. You can adjust the card to suit your group. You need various cards with different question configurations.

There are many variations on these items, but it works better if your cards are different from each other. It works even if you only rearrange the blocks but add some different items to keep it interesting.

Break the Ice

Why You Play – This game will give you various ways to warm up your attendees and is especially good for people who do not usually interact with others.

What You Need – You need name tags, felt markers, and a sponge ball for this game.

How to Play – Each attendee needs to think of a nickname. It can be one they have used or something new. They need to write it on an index card and a stick on name tag that should be turned face down. You need to collect the cards and read the nicknames aloud while the attendees try to guess who belongs to each name tag. When the person is identified, they should put the name tag on for all to see.

Tips and Suggestions – Allocate a set amount of time and keep a tight rein on the attendees. This is only to break the ice and should not run into your meeting time. Make sure that appropriate questions are being asked. The game can easily get out of hand so the leader or facilitator needs to control the time and questions.

Get to Know Each Other

Why You Play – This game allows people to get acquainted and can help you form business teams and partnerships.

How to Play – Divide the attendees into pairs. Some of the possible reasons to pair the two attendees can be that they never met before, work in different areas, have different jobs, have different backgrounds, share similar ideas, or they may have different ideas. Give the pairs a few minutes to get to know each other. Let them have some time alone. Give them a list of questions to discuss. These are some ideas, but you can use any questions to get them thinking.

- Why are you in the meeting?

- What is your favorite part of your job?

- What is your least favorite part of your job?

- What is the most important part of your job?

- What is the least important part of your job?

- Describe your job and work environment.

- Do you share any interests or background?

- Explain your successes.

- Are there any specific failures that you are willing to mention?

- What would you be doing if you weren't at work?

- What problems do you feel are unique to you?

- What problems do you feel are common with others?

Assign each pair a task that they can work on together so they can contribute to the meeting. If the pairs work together well, you might consider pairing them up on a permanent basis. Keep an open mind when you decide whom to pair. Sometimes the most unlikely pairs can accomplish the most together.

Make Some Changes – Attendees can be paired in larger groups of three or four. Have each attendee prepare a short bio to share.

Group Resume

Why You Play – This will help group members get acquainted and can help them see how their skills and experience complement each other.

How to Play – Divide attendees into groups of three to six members. Remind them that each member has beneficial experience that should be acknowledged. Let them brag about their skills and use these details to create a resume for the group. The attendees then create a resume that represents the group as a team. They can include:

- Education

- Knowledge about agenda subject matter

- Years of experience

- Business positions they held

- List professional skills and experience

- Include major accomplishments

- Publications or articles they published

- Include hobbies, talents

The individual groups can pick one person to present their resume to the group.

Make Some Changes – Prepare blank resume list and let the attendees complete. The attendees can interview each other to complete the resume.

I Am Here

Why You Play – An easy way for a lot of people to learn about each other quickly.

How to Play – Have each attendee stand up and tell the group their name, their occupation, where they are from, how long they have been in their job or profession, to state one of their beliefs, to give one opinion and one priority in the life. These are just a few of the possibilities. You might create a list and pass out questions to each attendee and ask them some different questions.

In Sync

Why You Play – You need your meeting attendees to work together, and this activity helps people learn to work with each other. They must learn about each other's strengths and weaknesses to work together.

How to Play – Challenge the attendees to sing a simple song together. Give them the words and let them go. You can challenge them to develop a short story together. Each attendee can add one sentence. This can get some interesting results. Pass a ball to the group and see how quickly they can pass it around without dropping it. Use LEGOs™ to build a project. Each person adds one or two pieces and sees what develops. These are a number of ways the group can work together and learn a team mentality. It is best to use only one of these at a time.

Quick Bits

Why You Play – Here is a quick and easy way to get to know others.

What You Need – No supplies are needed.

Tips and Suggestions – Each person is given 30 second to tell others about themselves, their job, and responsibilities. If they have time left, they can add information about their family and hobbies. At 30 seconds, the person beside them (clockwise) will have their 30 seconds. It is good to give the attendees an example of how this is done. Find a bell or buzzer to indicate their time is up. Another variation is to allow the person to use 10–15 words to explain the same information.

Scavenger Hunt

Why You Play – This game helps attendees learn to work together to reach a common goal.

How to Play – Distribute five to ten statements and have attendees find someone who fits the description. See the example on the next page.

SCAVENGER HUNT	
Find someone who (fill in the blanks):	**Name**
Likes	
Knows how to use a	
Thinks about	
Specializes in	
Has a collection of	
Believes that _____ _____ is bad.	
Just read a book about	
Has a good way to	
Owns four	

The attendees need to take the statements and circulate around the room. They are responsible to find people who fit each statement and need to complete the statement. When most of the answers are completed, collect the papers and you can award a small prize. Depending on your time frame, you may ask people about some of the most interesting things they learned.

Make Some Changes – You can allow enough time for everyone to find all the answers. Each attendee can talk with one person and get answers to all the questions.

Tell Us Who You Are

Why You Play – This is another way to help attendees get to know each other.

What You Need – Paper and writing utensils.

How to Play – Have each attendee write down two or three questions they would ask a person they just met. It is more fun if they are creative. They should wander around the room and exchange questions and answers with others. It is more effective if they talk to people they do not already know. Give them 5 to 10 minutes to gather information. Each attendee should stand one at a time and have others tell the group what they just learned. It is a fun way to share information with new acquaintances.

Tips and Suggestions – Keep things moving and keep an eye on the time. If someone stands and no one speaks up, ask the attendee to tell the group something interesting.

As you get more experience, you will come up with ideas of your own, and there are all sorts of ways to customize these ideas to work for your groups. The important thing is to have fun and help your attendees get acquainted and learn to work together.

8

CONDUCT EFFECTIVE MEETINGS

The leader is important to the success and effectiveness of the meeting, keeping the participants focused on its purpose and goals. Attendees' energy and attention need to stay on target. Let us analyze the components of your meeting.

MEETING COMPONENTS

These are the basic components of your meeting.

- **Content** – includes attitudes, expectations, experience, ideas, knowledge, myths, and opinions shared by the participants. Remember the content is not limited to the information that you present.

- **Participation** – How do the attendees interact with each other? Their feelings, attitudes, and expectations will have an impact on their willingness to cooperate, listen, and participate. Will the meeting have an "open" feeling?

- **Organization** – includes the way your agenda and information are organized to help you accomplish your goals for the meeting.

A good leader will keep an eye on each of these elements of the meeting. The leader needs to gauge the progress being made and steer the attendees in the right direction. These three components are critical to maintaining an effective meeting. Some participants may offer direction but ultimately the leader must oversee the meeting.

Successful and effective leaders can analyze what is happening, decide what action needs to be taken to keep the meeting on track, and move to the purpose. Below is a list of elements of the meeting that need to be monitored.

Content

These are the elements of your meeting's content.

- **Stay on Topic** – The leader and participants need to stay on topic.

- **Spur Participants to Action** – When you need participants, the leader needs to encourage and generate participation from attendees.

- **Evaluate all Points of View** – Your meeting is effective by your noting each point of view presented to the group.

- **Plan of Action** – The group needs to develop a way to handle issues being discussed or problems that need solutions.

- **Review** – A quick summary of topics can be valuable for your participants. Review the high points to ensure that all attendees understand what was discussed and any decisions that were finalized.

Participation

Participation is important to the success of your meeting. Use your judgment to determine who should attend.

- **Monitor** – Keep track of the people who participate and contribute to the meeting. Adjust the attendees to make your future meetings more successful.

- **Support** – Offer the needed support for your attendees, especially important for people who need to contribute to the discussion but who may be shy or hesitant. Make sure they know that you are there to help.

- **Encourage** – Be supportive to key people who offer their comments and details. You may need to ask quiet people to share their thoughts. One way to do this without undue pressure is to talk with them during a break and then call on them to speak. Never be pushy.

- **Difference of Opinion** – Any time you assemble a group of people, there will be differences and conflict. Effective leaders can keep these potential disruptions to a minimum. However, some differences will help the group generate more possible solutions and thoughts for your agenda topics. Do not discourage useful differences, but maintain control of the situation. A truly effective leader can maintain control without being obvious about it.

- **Reactions** – Watch the reactions of your attendees. How do various people react to the comments and suggestions? Can you use these reactions to your advantage? Sometimes a person's reaction will give you an idea about who should work on various projects or which attendees would work well together.

- **Feedback** – Feedback can work both ways. There are times when you need to offer feedback to attendees and you should encourage the attendees to give their feedback about the meeting content, format, and execution. After they give feedback, the leader needs to evaluate it to make needed adjustments in the meetings.

Organization

All events need to be organized, and your meeting is no different. Your agenda is the first step in being organized. Here is a list of the organizational elements of your meeting.

- **Agenda** – We discussed how to compile your agenda in Chapter 5.

- **Be Clear** – Make the purpose and goals of the meeting clear. Attendees can be more helpful when they know what needs to be done.

- **Assign Roles** – Each attendee needs to know what is expected of them. Some people will have more responsibilities, but each person needs to contribute something.

- **Time** – It is critical to keep the meeting within the proposed time frame. This shows that you prepared thoroughly and are maintaining control of the meeting.

- **Have a Plan** – The leader needs to develop a plan for presenting and distributing data, analyzing that data, finding options, sorting through feedback and suggestions, and making final decisions.

- **Ground Rules** – We talked about establishing and enforcing ground rules earlier. Review them occasionally to make sure they are effective.

WHO WILL CONDUCT THE MEETING?

The leader could be the most important person in a meeting. The chair will perform the following tasks:

- Call the meeting
- Understand the purpose and goals for the meeting
- Create the agenda and be familiar with the topics to be covered
- Pick all participants
- Lead the meeting

There are some cases where a meeting chair will be chosen based on who the person knows. This is NOT the best way to pick the person who will control the meeting. A person should be chosen because of qualifications and experience. The chair has the greatest power to make a meeting succeed or to mess it up. When the chair is unprepared or unqualified, the meeting is a disaster.

This person needs to have the appropriate leadership skills. Self confidence is an important trait for meeting leaders, but a large ego is not needed and can cause problems. Some of the key personality traits of an effective meeting chair include:

- Objectivity

- Consideration

- Ethical Behavior and Attitude

A leader who displays these qualities will build confidence in the attendees and lead to a successful meeting. A good leader will choose attendees with something to contribute, leading to a mutual respect and contributing to an effective meeting.

Successful meeting leaders need to be masters of multitasking, controlling the meeting, gauging the conversation, looking for problems or people who may be getting out of control, and many other situations at the same time.

When the leader is faced with a problem, he or she must be able analyze the positive and negative outcomes of their actions quickly and make a decision. The person needs to be prepared for potential fallout from people who may not like the decisions. Keep in mind that attendees who do not like the chair's decisions may indicate they feel the leader is dogmatic, unfriendly, self centered, and impatient. This reaction is not an indication of the leader's attitude but is merely the sign of an unhappy attendee.

Maintaining Control

Problems will crop up within any group of people—one key reason the meeting leader needs to maintain control. There are times when he or she will be called on to resolve disputes. Here are some tips to help settle some of these situations.

- Can you find mutual ground to bring the opposing people closer?

- Discuss possible ways to settle disagreements.

- Discuss the specific elements in dispute, avoid broad statements that are irrelevant to the issues being considered.

- Give each side an equal amount of time to voice their concerns.

- Make each side clearly state their point of view and their differences.

- When there is one side that is obviously right, steer the discussion that way.

- Find a way to state an individual opinion that highlights the best of both sides.

- When a debate is not going anywhere, end it.

CASE STUDY

There are many shy people in the business world who may feel they are not qualified to conduct a meeting. I spoke with Hope Clark who wrote a popular book for writers called *The Shy Writer*. She offers many tips and suggestions for shy people to function in groups and be able to promote themselves or their business. Below you will find suggestions she offers for shy people who are called upon to lead group discussions or take the lead in business.

"Professional peers and adversaries consider shyness a weakness. As shy as I am, however, my business affiliates never considered me so. I was an administrative director for a small federal agency for 10 years. I managed human resources, procurement, and budget-services all the other managers needed, argued about, and vied for when resources were limited. Managers approached me slicker than butter and meaner than snakes, but most of them received the same attention from me. I listened.

"Some thought my silence was patience. Some considered it arrogance. Bottom line was I hated to argue with people. I disliked bantering words, and in my world, the subject matter often meant debate. For a shy person, this was the path of least resistance. Most people began to interpret my silence as a skill. I called it wearing people down and avoiding confrontation.

"People presented their predicament or pitched their cause to me. I listened, took notes, and pondered my response. The conversations took fewer words, and the other person realized I heard every word. A shy person is a honed listener, and listening is a forgotten art. An extrovert is composing his next sentence and barely listening. An introvert is listening so he can speak to the fact in as few words as possible. This trait comes across to others as wisdom, tact, and patience.

"While I did not banter, I did speak when necessary. Meetings still require participation. Since I did not speak for speaking's sake, people heard my message. A wordy presentation loses its meaning. Fewer words mean a more pointed delivery—a point drilled home.

"Shy people think through their words before speaking, an asset that often allows them to spend less time in the limelight.

Painfully shy people can reduce their meeting discomfort by doing the following:

1. **Prepare in advance.** The more comfortable you are with your material, the easier the delivery and participation.

2. **Speak on the phone or to a friend.** You can call it warming up, but a shy person can chatter to someone comfortable and warm up the voice and the adrenaline before a meeting. I often advise writers giving interviews or calling editors to call up a friend and talk about the kids, the weather, or current events, and then while the blood is still rushing, pick up the phone and call the person they dread calling.

3. **Dress to impress.** Clothes empower. The listener pays more attention and the presenter feels more confident.

4. **Visuals.** Call it easy communication or hiding behind a prop, visuals make message delivery easier for the shy person. Not all eyes watch the speaker, and the well-designed visual speaks for the shy person. For some people, that simply means a polished name tag. I have name tags with my **FundsforWriters.com** logo and my name, C. Hope Clark. I wear the brand colors of green and black for money and ink, well-known needs of the struggling writer. These simple items break the ice and reduce conversation, often leading to the other person to take the conversation and run with it. I insert my words as needed. The person walks away thinking he was treated professionally because I intently listened to him. The less need for introduction enabled us to communicate easier and simply.

C. Hope Clark
Editor FundsforWriters, www.fundsforwriters.com
Creator of amazing market ebooks for writers!
Writer's Digest 101 Best Web Sites for Writers - 2001 through 2006

WOMEN IN CHARGE

There may be some problems for male attendees when a woman is in charge. I have conducted many meetings with male and female attendees and did not have problems, but I approached the meeting as a professional. My attitude helped to eliminate gender bias. A meeting with more men than women may cause problems for a woman in charge, a sorry fact of life in some businesses.

Of course, not all men share this viewpoint, but women who plan to conduct a meeting need to be prepared for the possibility. Interestingly enough, women in attendance may be critical of women too, but for different reasons. An attractive and confident woman who leads a meeting and pretends there will not be any bias is doing herself and the attendees an injustice.

This is not the only bias we find in business. Some others include:

- A younger person being made supervisor of an older, more experienced staff member.

- Race influencing how situations are handled within a business.

- A larger person choosing not to work for a smaller person.

I am not condoning these situations, but you need to consider them when planning a meeting and deciding who will attend and who will be in charge.

In a perfect world no one would care, but be honest with yourself that people behave differently when there are overt differences among them particularly if one group feels another group is acting superior, victimized, or deferential toward them. How many times have you seen men holding out chairs for other men? That is just one example, but there are others.

Eliminate Unnecessary Distractions

I was recently involved in a networking forum in which one participant, a woman, posted a message that she has great looking legs and will

CASE STUDY

Leading any organization should be a function and measure of competency and ability to motivate. Whether female or male, legitimate contributions result from being educated on the issues, striving to articulate your position and working in a progressive mode with colleagues.

Women can set the tone for the way their work is received. It is critical that women be self-assured with the understanding that their work is as valuable as their male counterparts. The blend of male/female contributions in any organization is a tremendous asset. The person in charge must exude confidence and egalitarian leadership skills that will garner respect.

Modern society expects women to take leadership roles. Women have historically performed the most difficult job: running a household and raising children. We have all begun to realize that many of the skills used successfully at home are assets in the workplace.

Lorie Smith
Former School Board Leader
Waynesboro, VA City Councilwoman

continue to wear short skirts to business meetings to get the upper hand. That sort of thinking trivializes everyone's contributions to the workplace. A business meeting should be focused on legitimate business.

A Matter of Emotion

The opposite problem is when a woman is appointed just because she is a woman. Man or woman, the best person for the job should be appointed. Leading a meeting is far too important to be left to the person without qualifications.

EFFECTIVELY MANAGE THE MEETING

Most people are aware that many ineffective meetings are held every day because their leaders are unacquainted with meeting skills or unprepared. Consider these facts about meetings from the book *How to Hold Successful Meetings* by Paul R. Timm, PhD.

- More than 70 percent of executives feel that most the meetings they attend are a waste of time. However, 67 percent said they attended more meetings this year, than they did last year. (*Success* magazine)

- In *How to Win the Meeting*, Frank Snell reports that executives spend 75 percent of their time in meetings.

- The higher executives spend more of their time in meetings. This means the highest paid people in companies are spending most of their time in meetings, a colossal waste of money if the meetings are not effective.

- A Xerox Learning Center advertisement states that senior executives spend at least five hours in meetings, each day.

Each of these facts shows why people need more interesting and effective meetings. Here is an example of something you should never do.

The meeting is scheduled to begin at 10 a.m., but the leader is not there. Minutes click by, but the leader does not arrive. No one in attendance has any idea where the leader is or when he would arrive. Eventually, at 10:20 a.m., the leader rushes in the door with a big pile of papers. He lays the papers on the table and simply says, "We need to get busy. There is a lot of work to do today."

I have been in meetings that began like this with no apology, rude and unprofessional behavior. If you will be late, call to let attendees know when you will be there. Otherwise, the meeting starts on a negative note.

- Another issue is choosing someone to make rules for the group who does not lead the meeting. It is not that complicated to run an effective meeting, but the leader needs to maintain control over the meeting and participants, enforcing rules the group has approved, and focus completely on the meeting rather than outside problems or issues.

These tips make it easier to lead an effective meeting. Are you the sort of person who can accomplish these activities? If not, who should lead the meeting? Or what do you need to learn to conduct an effective meeting?

- **Be Prepared** – Have your agenda in hand. It should be researched and thorough. Any reports, handouts, and visual aids need to be ready before the meeting. Other key attendees should be alerted to be prepared, and the leader needs to have a plan to weave the parts of the meeting together.

- **Use the Procedures** – The leader needs to present all information, evaluate and analyze the data, lead the group to a decision, and then move the group to action. These steps need to be fresh in mind at all times. These are the things that need to be accomplished and the leader needs to plan how to implement these steps.

- **Agenda** – We discussed the agenda in detail earlier, but here are a couple of other reasons you need an agenda. A thorough agenda will save time, can serve as a checklist to keep the leader and meeting on track, should be available to all attendees before the meeting, and needs to have an underlying message that it contains valuable information. To make the agenda more recognizable, keep to the same colors, format, shape, and size. When you follow the prepared agenda, your attendees know what to expect when they look at the agenda. This is a big step toward helping attendees prepare accurately for meetings.

- **Where to Sit** – This is something we discussed earlier. Sometimes you need to assign people to specific seats so that you prevent disruptions. Seating can help you see how some individuals work together and that others should not work together. See Chapter 6 for the best room layout and seat people accordingly.

- **Introductions** – When you plan to encourage discussion and interaction, it is good to introduce the people in attendance. Mention their name, job, expertise, and pertinent background. This is courteous and puts everyone on a level playing field because they can identify others in the meeting.

- **Put it All on the Table** – All specifics need to be presented to the group before any effective decisions can be made. If you share only some of the details, you cannot get the full benefit from the group you assembled. Make sure all background information and other specifics are considered before a final decision is made or a final vote is taken.

- **Keep on keeping On** – It is critical to keep the meeting moving. When the meeting slows down, people get bored, uninterested, and distracted. Here are some techniques for a brisk meeting:

  o Have your questions prepared ahead of time and keep them handy.

  o Watch the clock subtly but know how much time you have left.

  o Stay on Topic. Keep your comments relevant to the meeting topics and keep the participants on topic.

  o Sum it Up. At strategic intervals in the meeting, briefly summarize what has been discussed and decided up to that point. to show the meeting is accomplishing something.

- **Be Balanced** – An effective and unbiased meeting leader will listen to the positive and negative thoughts. They will give all sides a chance to talk and will not play favorites.

- **The End** – Your meeting needs a definite conclusion. If the meeting was called to solve problems, attendees need to reach a decision or resolution before the meeting is over. Find a way to let the group know the meeting is over and then adjourn.

- **Agree to Disagree** – We will discuss disagreements in more detail, but the meeting leader needs to monitor arguments and fights. Healthy disagreement is great for brainstorming, but the leader needs to know when to break up a fight and not let it get out of control. If the comments become personal attacks, those need to be stopped immediately.

- **Open Your Mind and Ears** – It is important to open your mind and your ears. The leader needs to listen to what is being said. Listen to the participants and keep an eye on what is being said. Effective communication is key and we will discuss that in much more detail in Chapter 11.

FACILITATING MEETINGS

One key element of facilitating a meeting is to stay in control without smothering participants. A meeting may start out fine without a facilitator but it will not stay on track. It is easy to start following the agenda. However, with no one to keep attendees focused, direct and oversee questions and discussions the meeting will begin to drift. We've all seen meetings where the people who talk the most take up much of the meeting time. This does not mean they have the most useful information, just that they talk a lot. They might bring up old stories and unrelated issues that do nothing to help the group accomplish the goals for the meeting. It will also drain the enthusiasm and energy from the attendees without getting to the subject of the meeting.

Another problem is that some attendees will be eliminated from the conversation and discussion. The leader may not call on them because they may not speak as eloquently or directly as others in the group. These people may stop making the effort and simply withdraw from the discussion. The leader should be careful not to give negative responses when quiet or shy participants do make an effort. I was in a training meeting one time and the leader had several issues with me. I was a manager and assistant, but not a doctor, and I am a woman. Apparently those were two strikes against me. He would not call on me. Two doctors were seated next to me and one noticed I was not being called on. He suggested that I pass my questions to him. I did and all my questions were answered. It was not the ideal situation, but it worked.

CASE STUDY

If you would like to get the most out of your business meeting you really must make the event challenging and interesting for your participants. As a retail store manager, I conducted meetings on a monthly basis to keep the staff up-to-date on store business. It was my goal, as manager, to ensure that we consistently increased sales over both the previous year and each month in the current year. I wanted to show the owners of the company a constant climb in sales and a consistent decrease in inventory shortages because of shoplifting. This could not be accomplished without motivated employees.

How do you turn a meeting into a successful event? In my case, I made it fun. Most often my employees were teenagers who did not earn commissions on each sale but were paid by the hour. I created my own incentives that I announced in each meeting jobs well done and previous goals accomplished. Instead of a formal meeting with a set agenda we all sat around a circle on the floor and brainstormed. They felt part of the overall success of the store because I implemented their ideas. Many of the employees weren't accustomed to such a personal approach to making the store successful but were used to boring, dry, formal meetings where they were never asked their opinion and were instead told what to do.

By including them in the business of the store I created "one big happy family" with an informal open door policy and they worked even harder to make the store successful. They no longer had to submit a written request for a meeting with me even though I still had to do that with my supervisor.

In the end, I was able to double sales over the previous year in each place that I worked by involving my employees during fun, engaging, informal meetings where I offered my own incentives as manager, asked for and implemented their opinions about running the store, and made them a part of a growing family. These monthly meetings were key in retaining successful, loyal employees who worked hard to make the store a success.

Melissa Alvarez
Business Owner and Award-Winning Novelist and Nonfiction Author
www.MelissaA.com

Too Much Control

Facilitators need to be careful not to wield a heavy hand over the meeting. Experienced leaders know the right times to let the group talk freely and when to exert more control. It is a fine line, but it can be learned with practice. These are some signs that the facilitator is using too much control.

- Strictly adhering to parliamentary procedure

- The leader or facilitator talks too much

- Too little participation from the other attendees

- The leader is bossy and overly confident and pushy

- The leader is overly aggressive and domineering

Exhibiting any of these traits is not in the best interest of the meeting. Each attendee should be there for a reason and each needs to participate. This is especially critical in problem solving meetings.

Facilitators should not micromanage meetings. If the agenda is prepared properly and the attendees are given time to prepare, there should not be any reason to micromanage the meeting or the group. Have you ever noticed how attendees seem to tune out things when they are being controlled too much? They feel manipulated or useless, and no one responds well in these situations.

Some unruly groups may need a "heavy handed" approach. However, it is not the best way to handle the meeting when you need attendees to participate and share their thoughts. Below are some tips for steering your meetings.

- Teach all group members how to facilitate.

- Learn how to speak and manage a meeting in a positive way and teach this to each person in the group.

- One person needs to be assigned to facilitate each meeting. You can assign different people, but be sure to have one person in charge.

- The meeting leader and the facilitator need to be two different people and two distinct roles. This can also work as a way to check each other and to keep the meeting on track and running effectively.

Train Group Members to Facilitate

Facilitating a meeting is not some mysterious secret that only a Yoda-like creature would know. Effective facilitators took the time to learn the "secrets" to a successful meeting. It is good for any group that has periodic or frequent meetings to have a number of people trained to facilitate. It does not hurt for each member of your group to learn how to facilitate. Keep in mind that people trained to facilitate will also make great participants. They understand what makes a meeting successful and will contribute to the discussions. Below are some of the skills any meeting facilitator should possess.

- Keep the group members involved and have high energy and enthusiasm.

- Listen well and bring the meeting back to the main subject when it drifts off course.

- Encourage all attendees to participate without putting them on the spot or making them feel uncomfortable. Keep in mind that people communicate in different ways, and an effective facilitator should be able to work with all of them.

- When attendees are disruptive, the facilitator needs to take control of the situation.

- Be alert to attendees who have a "hidden agenda" and squelch this behavior.

- Keep a sense of humor and learn to use it effectively in the meeting—tough to do? Yes, but it only requires practice and learning from others' examples.

- Pay special attention to concerns or needs of the newest group members.

- An effective facilitator must remain objective. This helps to keep the discussion on track and encourages attendees to share differing viewpoints and thoughts.

- Be forceful when needed, but do not be harsh. Knowing when to interrupt and when to stand back and let the attendees discuss issues.

- No matter what happens, the facilitator must do what is needed to see the meeting reaches its goals. Doing so means putting the interest of the group and the meeting ahead of any personal interests.

- It is important to create an atmosphere where the attendees feel safe, so that they can be comfortable expressing their creative side.

Facilitator Skills

Certain specific skills can help build your group and make the attendees stronger. A few of these skills include:

- **Be Clear** – You may need to elaborate on ideas and suggestions to make sure all attendees understand the details.

- **Get Started** – When problems arise, offer suggestions on how they can be resolved. If the discussion lags, the facilitator needs to nudge the participants by offering additional details or calling on individuals who have information pertinent to the discussion.

- **Inspire** – Sometimes your group members will offer suggestions that are great raw material that only needs to be formed into a useful idea. I often tell people that it can be easy to make an initial suggestion, but more is needed to make the idea workable.

- **Moods** – Every group of people will have a certain mood. The facilitator needs to learn to gauge the mood and take action to improve the mood when needed.

- **Positive** – It is important to be encouraging and respond promptly to concerns and questions. You can also keep things positive by treating all attendees in the same way.

- **Sum it Up** – Compile all information and determine where there is agreement and where there are disagreements. It is also important to make recommendations about what should be approved and what should not. Move the group toward a final decision or resolution.

- **Talk** – All attendees need to work to communicate with each other in an open and honest atmosphere.

- **Time's Up** – Timing includes starting and ending on time. You might have a timekeeper in the group to help you keep track of the time.

- **Watch** – Watch the attendees for potential problems and take breaks as needed.

- **Work Together** – Groups need someone to be a mediator and to help them explore their differences and concerns. Most differences can be worked out; it just takes patience and a clear head.

Who Should Train Facilitators

Your first priority should be to find someone in the group who has facilitating experience. If so, that person could be your first choice. It would be good to become familiar with their facilitating skills before you ask them to train other people. There are training sessions that group members can attend. For large companies, it might be best to have a trainer come to you.

Group members will learn more through practice after they have learned some things from a trainer. Any time you have a new person facilitating, it is best to inform the group and ask them to be patient, helpful, and understanding. The facilitator will get better with practice. During any practice, someone needs to be assigned to take notes of things the facilitator needs to work on. These notes should include good points and bad points. Right after the meeting, this person should speak with the facilitator trainee to review the things they need to practice. Again, focus on the positive things, too.

Leader Compared to Facilitator

The meeting leader and facilitator are not the same position. It is much better to have two different people handle these roles. Many leaders have specific interest in the meeting goals and this makes it impossible or difficult for them to remain neutral when discussing problems or situations.

When you have both a leader and facilitator for the meeting, the leader can get more involved in the discussion and problem solving elements without having to worry about details of handling the meeting. However, the leader is ultimately responsible for the outcome of the meeting even if there is a facilitator. The facilitator is only responsible to run the meeting correctly. It is also human nature that participants will open up more when the leader or boss is not running the meeting. An impartial facilitator lets people feel they can share their thoughts which should benefit the meeting.

With a facilitator the leader's responsibilities are altered. The leader can participate in the meeting more fully and is free to pay closer attention to the discussion and other details. The leader is not required to be neutral on meeting topics, but it will be more effective if the leader voices an opinion after others state their thoughts. If you have enough qualified people, a separate leader and facilitator make for a better quality meeting.

LEADERSHIP SKILLS

Here are essential skills of any meeting facilitator.

- **Listen** – It is important to listen to each person in the meeting for their choice words, the tone or inflection in their voice, the intent behind the words, and their body language as they speak.

- **Make it Clear** – It is effective to summarize the comments being made by the attendees, especially if they ramble or there are two points of view.

- **Develop the Group** – Watch the dynamics and growth of the group, determined by the group's background, size, tone, and how much the group is willing to learn and develop.

- **Procedures** – Be familiar with the tools the group can use in various situations. Where is the group in the process?

- **Manage Conflict** – The facilitator needs to find the appropriate times to step in when there are conflicts in the meeting. Conflicts can produce some great brainstorming but should not be allowed to go too far. An experienced facilitator knows what to do and when to do it.

- **Keep Records** – There needs to be a written record of the decisions made. Visual aids are also important in your meetings. They can be handouts, overhead projectors, or flip charts. It is up to the facilitator to find the best method to convey the information.

LOOK LIKE A LEADER

There are a number of things you can do to look like a leader. I've discussed some of these things below.

CASE STUDY

It is indeed true that effective leadership will set the tone for any organization. There are certain individuals who are progressive thinkers, have no problem with public speaking, and have skills that create good working environments. That being said, leadership skills develop with experience.

Having been a School Board leader for three years and now on the local City Council, there are many strategies I have developed that enable me to provide effective and appropriate leadership to my constituency. I have made it a priority to do significant research on all facets of the organization. A meaningful strategy I have implemented has been to meet individually with department heads for two purposes, (1) it begins to form solid relationships with personnel and (2) you become intimately informed as to the details of each organizational area.

Individuals in leadership roles must exude confidence and have control of all the information relative to the respective organization. It is also critical that leaders understand the "role" of the elected body or board. There are clear designations with respect to roles in most organizations. For example, City Councils in the State of Virginia have no direct role in administering personnel matters. Administration is the role of the city manager. Roles are defined. It is of paramount importance that leadership set the tone for the appropriate roles to be carried out by organizational boards.

As we observe well-run meetings, it is always noticeable when an individual in a leadership position demonstrates the ability to speak confidently, understand meeting protocols, perhaps *Roberts Rules of Order* and create an environment that vests everyone in the issues. Organizationally, it is always beneficial to provide appropriate recognition to staff and those contributing to matters that come before the board. Leadership skill discussion would not be complete without acknowledgment of the importance of communication.

Leaders should meet with their administrator on a prescribed schedule, i.e., mayor with city manager, school board leader with superintendent. This enables your leader to manage current issues as well as set your meeting agendas. Communication internally with your organization as well as externally to the community is extremely important. Decisions become much more defensible when everyone knows how and why they were made.

If you are involved in elected capacities, it is important to create good relationships with your local media. You, as the leader, can educate the media on the issues to aid them in their reporting. This is truly a service to your local community. However, there will be instances where you will be negatively scrutinized on your decisions; welcome to public service. Again, communication is key; education is key.

To summarize effective leadership:

1) Research your organization thoroughly.

2) Arrange to meet with personnel to gain a better understanding of their respective areas.

3) Communicate with your board members consistently.

4) Educate yourself in meeting protocols.

5) Educate your board as to their role.

6) Set a confident tone for your organization.

7) Nurture good relationships with the press.

Lorie Smith
Former School Board Leader
Waynesboro, VA City Councilwoman

Dress for Success

The way we look does make a difference in how we feel. It also affects how we project ourselves to others. People respond positively to people who appear self assured and enthusiastic. This means that it is important for you to analyze the way you look and then dress for success.

Here are some tips to create your meeting clothes.

- Color can have varied affects on people. Bold colors have a different effect than muted colors. Black, dark blue, gray, tan, brown, and similar colors can blend in with the background. However, red, green, blue, yellow, and brighter colors will make you stand out. Although bright colors are not all you need, they will help to instill excitement in your attendees and prepare them for the information to be shared. An easy and inexpensive way to accomplish this is as easy as adding a colorful scarf or other accessory to spice up your wardrobe.

- You should not dress too casually or in loose fitting clothes. Each of these things will give you a relaxed appearance and a flighty, fluttery look.

- Some ways to look more professional include pressed clothes, crisp collars and seams, and clothes that fit well to present a professional image and make the attendees see you as a leader.

- Traditional, widely accepted clothing gives you a professional appearance. Fads in clothing do not promote a professional image.

These are some basic tips to tailor your wardrobe and appearance to give you a professional image that will gain the respect and attention of your attendees.

Body Language

Your body language conveys much information to meeting attendees. Walk into the room with your head high and back straight and you instill confidence, showing that you are in charge. If you walk into a meeting with your head hanging low and looking timid, the meeting will get away from you. I found this fascinating chart in the book, *Running a Meeting That Works, Third Edition* by Robert F. Miller and Marilyn Pincus.

P – Posture – upright, not sagging. Capable

O – Obviously caring. Smiling, listening. Involved.

W – Walk tall. Do not drag your feet or slouch shoulders. Secure

E – Eye contact. Direct. Intent

R – Relaxed body, especially arms, hands, shoulders. Calm

What signals do you emit when you walk into a room? What can you do to be seen in a better light?

Which methods and techniques would work with your meeting? Are there other ways that you can use these ideas to make your meetings more effective?

9

ELEMENTS OF AN
EFFECTIVE MEETING

———

Scores of attendees complain about unproductive meetings. Some indicators of an unproductive meeting are:

- A rude boss

- Receiving conflicting information

- Impossible expectations for attendees

- Attendees tossed together in an illogical way

- Information is dispensed from leader to attendees, but leader is not willing to receive information

- Some attendees are narrow minded

- Disruptive attendees are not monitored or controlled

However, some great ways to promote productive meetings include encouraging attendees to collaborate, meeting in an open room that allows space to move around, and meet with people who want to accomplish something while there.

CASE STUDY: Making Meetings More Productive

It seems everyone is always in a meeting. What is really being accomplished, if anything? Some people feel important if they are in a meeting, but what are they doing in there?

If you are a manger and need to have meetings there are things you can do to make them much more productive. Some tips to have an effective, productive meeting that does not go on all day are:

- **Plan ahead** – create a schedule and stick to it!

- **Remove the chairs from the meeting room** – when you have to stand for your meeting you will find that you go over the issues at hand and move on to the next item much more quickly.

- **Remove or shut off the phones** – focus on why you are there; remove any distractions so you can effectively concentrate on the meeting points.

- **Do not serve food or snacks** – serving food causes a relaxed atmosphere that does not contribute to productivity.

- **Schedule your topics and give each one a time limit** – for example, Joe will talk about receivables and how we can improve them for 10 minutes. Then Mary will talk about health insurance for 15 minutes.

- **USE A KITCHEN TIMER!** – When the buzzer goes off the meeting is over. Get back to work.

If you find you are not able to cover everything, some topics may be covered without a meeting. Some ways you can get the word out to employees without having a meeting are by using memos.

Michelle Dunn, Author/Consultant
www.michelledunn.com

SHAKE THINGS UP

Are you dealing with people who only work with words and numbers? Sometimes, it is good to encourage them to open their minds and use a different method to analyze the information. Even if they do not have any artistic ability, sketching and drawing rough pictures could be beneficial. It is a way to tap into another part of the attendees' brains and generate some additional creativity because the group members are looking at the situation or issue from a different perspective and another angle.

It is also good to break things up for the attendees. If they seem stuck, offer a chance to stand up and walk around. Creativity cannot be forced effectively. Another thing is to give attendees a chance to use a flow chart or other visual aid to get ideas flowing.

At times the attendees need to talk to get the sketch done.

It is also possible to make alterations to this process. Attendees might want to use a series of transparencies, pictures, or sketches that can be overlaid or cut and pasted together. Each of these possibilities will help you reach the same result. This is not an exercise where you would be overly uptight or regimented. Give the participants some freedom and flexibility to solve the question.

Here are some ways to get your participants moving and boost productivity.

- Analyze the problem from a different perspective.
- Use a flow chart to illustrate the process or make changes to the process.
- Use a geographical map if location is an element.
- Set a timeline with time estimates to reach certain goals.
- Sketch possible floor plans or floor plan changes.
- Pie chart or graphs are a good way to illustrate more details.

MOTIVATE ATTENDEES

Motivation is critical to maintaining morale and participation. Unmotivated employees who dread attending meetings and have bad attitudes from the time they arrive until they leave are unpleasant for everyone to deal with.

Motivated attendees work harder to help the group reach its goals improving the situation for everyone in the meeting. A pleasant, hard working crew makes your job easier. Next would be, "How can I motivate my group?"

Create and Maintain Positive Attitudes

Attitudes influence how people feel about any task or topic and can stifle their participation.

These conditions affect participant's attitude.

- Their feelings and thoughts about something affect their reaction. When they think good things, they will feel positive. When they tell themselves bad things, they will have a negative attitude. This gives them the power to feel good or bad about something.

- Their state of mind has an impact. Its is affected by what they tell themselves. How do they react to their own feelings?

Thoughts are more powerful than we realize at times. When we do not like something or cannot do something, we avoid it. This thinking has a definite impact on your meeting attendee's productivity.

Positive and negative attitudes are powerful, so let us identify them:

- **Positive** – Sincere caring or love promotes helpful and beneficial actions.

- **Negative** – Fear and anger, with or without any basis leads to hurtful and defensive actions.

Find ways to motivate your team and avoid negativity. Negative, hurtful, and defensive thoughts cause bad attitudes and limit productivity.

A positive attitude improves the morale of your attendees. Have you been in a meeting with an unhappy person ? Even when the meeting is going well, one disgruntled attendee can make the meeting tasks a chore. The person can ruin a great day and stymie the productivity of the people near them.

It is important that the meeting leader and facilitator maintain a good attitude. Attitudes are contagious. Be enthusiastic about the tasks before the group.

Another thing that promotes positive attitudes is showing an interest in how actions on topics on your agenda will benefit your team members. Show them that you care about the group's success. There are simple things you can do that mean a lot to them and prove that you realize they are human beings with lives outside the office. Recognize their anniversary, birthday, children's birthdays, children's accomplishments, or anything else that involves them and their loved ones. You could assign a person to keep up with important dates and events for the purpose of recognizing these events in the group.

Motivation Prompts Productivity

In the last section we discussed productivity and the good news is that motivation and productivity work together. Your group will thrive in your meetings when you have a productive team taking the pressure off you and making it easier to plan for a good meeting.

Here are some tips to increase their productivity in your group:

- Your group will face problems from time to time. Encourage your attendees to offer solutions. They could offer ideas you can use or they might not. Either way, they are involved in solving the problem. Show that you value their thoughts and opinions.

- You might have competitions between the attendees to find solutions, but do not pit employees against each other in a negative way.

- Look for ways to make the group's duties easier and streamline the procedures. These ideas may be new ways to do things or may improve on your current procedures to achieve productivity because the duties will be handled faster and smoother.

- It is helpful to teach your attendees to understand the importance of maintaining and increasing productivity. You could even reward participants for ideas that save work and promote productivity.

CASE STUDY

There are only two types of meetings, "RAH RAH" meetings that pump up our staff and directive meetings that tackle problems.

Directive meetings are held to present ideas or implement a particular plan of action. I firmly believe that the *method* you use to present the idea or plan of action will ultimately lead to the success or failure of that idea!

My directive meetings begin by outlining the problem as I interpret it and then I ask for ideas from my employees for possible solutions.

Before the meeting, I have already considered many possible solutions and have usually decided which one I feel will work best. I also plan my responses to any possible suggestions for any ideas other than the one that I would like to see implemented. As employees present their solutions, I quickly present a situation to show that idea will not work. Eventually the employees' ideas reach the best solution to address the problem and I agree with them and approve their choice.

The plan of action to be used is not my idea, but theirs. Attendees will do their utmost to see that their plan of action is successful. I occasionally pay a reward to solidify their efforts.

You get more effort from a pat of the back than a directive from a superior.

Parmer Bradley, Owner
Bradley Insurance Services
Staunton, Virginia

Avoid Favoritism

Showing favoritism can cause problems in your meetings. Playing favorites will "unmotivate" your attendees. That is not a real word, but it gets my point across. As the meeting leader, you need to take the time and make the effort to motivate your staff. Showing favoritism will undo your efforts.

Some favoritism with attendees may not be a big deal, but it has negative repercussions. Do you want to risk turning the attitude of your attendees against you? You can avoid that by being able to substantiate any favoritism you show. There are good reasons to favor certain people: doing an outstanding job on a project, developing a new process for your tasks, or something else that benefits the company and your team.

Protect yourself from unfair accusations by having justification for the favoritism before you recognize employees. If you cannot justify it to yourself, there is no chance that your attendees will believe you. Recognizing participants for excelling at their tasks well can motivate them to continue to do well and motivate others to work harder. Recognition and proper favoritism can be motivating.

Encourage Improvement

Any managers like to see people their group or team making improvement. Attendee improvement means better productivity. You can encourage attendees to improve by motivating them. Most people want to do better, and your encouragement will help them.

People try to do better when someone supports them. Show support for your meeting participants and let them know you are available when they have problems. This can motivate them to take chances and can help them improve. As they improve, they become more valuable in your meetings.

If attendees come to you about things they do not know, how do you handle it? Would you help him or her learn more or shrug it off and have someone else do the work? When employees come to you about a task, it is usually because they want to improve. Remember they can become bored when you do not challenge them and encourage them to do more. Your offer to help them improve is motivating. They want to do more and strive for more responsibility.

Listen when your participants want to do more. Encourage them to accept additional responsibilities. Are there training seminars they can attend? Is there someone in your group who can teach them? It is important to find solutions quickly and keep their momentum going.

The best participants will get tired of being taken for granted. I've seen this happen with group members who are not recognized for their efforts. The leaders appreciate them but need to express these thoughts. Tell the attendees on a regular basis that you appreciate them so that they will continue to do a consistent and superior job. When attendees make a special effort, take the opportunity to praise their work. People never get tired of being praised. If they do an outstanding job at five consecutive meetings, tell them you appreciate that effort each day. It takes little effort to say "thank you" and "good job," but you will reap the rewards by motivating your participants.

Less Than Expected and Needed

You can destroy morale and ruin motivation by allowing substandard work. When attendees do substandard work, the situation needs to be addressed. You must be able to count on consistent participation from your attendees. This means you must deal with work that does not meet your standards and expectations.

Your first priority is to explain your expectations to the group. Be sure they understand the standards that you insist they maintain. They cannot work up to your requirements unless they understand them. Every leader must set standards for their employees' performance. The standards can be a part of the group's ground rules.

Explain the quality of work that you need from your group. If they have questions, give them a complete explanation and help them understand what is expected. When they do well, motivate them by recognizing their successes. Point out what you liked about their work. If others hear, it will improve their performance as well. However, when you need to reprimand someone, do that in private.

When attendees do less than you expect, explain how to fix existing problems. The attendee learns more when they make the changes. If someone else fixes the mistakes, the original attendee does not learn and cannot improve, discouraging all attendees.

Give attendees a chance to ask questions and share their thoughts. They may try to divert your attention to another issue, but make them deal with problems. Once they understand the problems, form a plan to improve their performance and participation. It is advisable to establish a timetable for improvement. Follow-up to be sure they are working on the plan and remind them of the deadline if necessary.

These tips will help you motivate attendees who show less initiative while keeping your more successful participants motivated. You need motivated and positive participants to have effective meetings.

Games to Motivate

Share Warm Fuzzies

Why Play – This is a great game to help people learn to realize people need positive feedback and to help them learn to give positive feedback.

How to Play –

- Explain to the group how important positive feedback is for everyone.

- Everyone in the group needs to pair up with someone else.

- Each person needs to find something positive about their partner.

- Have them share a simple and brief positive comment.

- Ask the Participants a Few Questions

  o Do they share positive comments with others? How often?

  o Do you hear other people sharing positive comments? How often?

  o Do you receive positive comments? How often?

  o Is there a reason we do not offer more positive comments to each other?

A Little Better

Why Play – This is a great way to show attendees that they can always do at least a little bit better.

How to Play –

- You need a volunteer.

- Have them stretch their arm as high as possible on the wall. Find some way to mark how far they reach. You can use a chalkboard, a peg board or a piece of paper attached to the wall. Mark the highest point they reach.

- Have them stretch their arm again and really stretch. Mark the new spot they reach. It is almost always higher than the first mark. If they do not reach higher, encourage them more.

- Ask the attendees for their conclusions.

- Ask the Participants a Few Questions –

  o Are you hesitant to do something new and unusual?

  o Is there anything we could do to help alleviate your concerns?

  o Are there ways you could improve or increase your work by just 10 percent?

  o How can we help make that possible?

My Idea of Success Is...

Why Play – This game is a way to help people see how their values and the values of others change as their situations and experience change.

How to Play – Remind the attendees that our idea of "success" is highly individualized. Ask two or three people what their idea of success is, and ask the following questions.

- When you were in elementary school, what was your idea of success?

- What made a person a success in your eyes at that time?

- How did you define success when you entered the work world?

- Is the amount of money someone makes the only way to define success?

- If not, what else is included?

- Do you see yourself as a success? Why or why not?

PRESENTATIONS

Keep in mind that some people spend far too much time on presentations. When you consider doing a presentation, ask yourself whether a report or memo would accomplish the same thing without having a meeting. If so, then create a report and circulate it to all concerned.

Many presentations are poorly prepared, and the delivery leaves much to be desired. A well crafted report is much more beneficial than a poor presentation. The bad presentations are a waste of time (money) and belittle the presenter's credibility.

You may be wondering what makes it so difficult to make an effective presentation. Some people think that you only need to stand up and state the facts to the group. That is the first sign of trouble. Stating the facts is only the beginning. It is critical to make sure you say the information in a way that conveys the correct details to the attendees. Communication is important in presentations and you must convey the right information. One way to realize that the attendees understand is by watching their reactions and listening to what they have to say in response.

When you develop your presentation, consider the attendees' reaction. The presentation needs to be designed in a way to fit into your meeting and to get the points across to the participants. It is important to ask yourself: who, what, when, why, where, how, and how many. Make sure your presentation answers all these questions in an effective way.

The Audience

The first step in creating an effective presentation is to get to know your attendees. It is important that you know the people who will hear your presentation to convey the information effectively. Ask yourself the following questions.

- Who will be in the audience?

- What sort of people are they?

- What do they need and expect from you?

- What do they need and expect from this presentation?

- Do they have any knowledge of the subject?

- What additional details do they need to understand the topic?

- What terminology will they understand?

- Does the presentation need to be specific or can it be generalized?

- What do you need them to do with the information they get from the presentation?

- What do they think about me?

- How do I need to present the information to get the points through to them?

These questions will help you get started with your presentation. You have expectations for the presentation, but so do the attendees. The questions will also help you to tailor the information for the attendees to present the details they need and to avoid duplicating things they already know.

Prepare Your Presentation

Your presentation needs to communicate the relevant information to the attendees. Some of the information will need to overlap to move from one point to another and to tie it together. First, determine the main points that you want and need to convey. Do not try to cover too much information in a presentation or you will not be able to cover the information sufficiently. After you have decided on the main points, list the key ideas included in each main point.

Handouts can be helpful for your attendees, but keep them simple and short. They can be sent out before the meeting with the agenda or after the meeting. When you distribute handouts during the meeting, attendees can be absorbed in reading these and will not pay attention to your presentation. Attendees can review the information and be prepared for your presentation. They can also bring the handout to the meeting and make notes during your talk.

It is important to keep your presentation within a schedule; time your talk, adding time for any questions. Keep the information limited to the time available. Keep the presentation as short as possible but cover the important information.

The way your information is organized can make a big difference in how effective your presentation will be. Some of the things you need to mention at the beginning include:

- The reason for the presentation.
- Tell them how you organized your presentation.
- Explain what action you expect them to take.

One thing that will hinder your presentation is to share only your viewpoint or your thoughts; it will be much more effective when you include thoughts from other people. You can pose questions at the meeting or send questions to particular people before your presentation, allowing them time to prepare a response, saving time at the meeting.

You can encourage people to help you succeed by asking for their thoughts and suggestions. Involve them in the process and it will be more effective. You can make statements about the conclusions you have made and have others offer their suggestions for improvement. Diversified information to develop your proposals can be beneficial for the group and will make your presentation more successful.

When to Accept Questions

Questions can be asked at the beginning, the middle, or the end of your presentation. Here are some ways to determine when questions would be most appropriate.

Beginning

Questions at the beginning require that the attendees be familiar with the topic. This is the best way for them to ask intelligent and specific questions at the beginning. Questions at the start will help you know what the attendees are thinking. It is also good for you to have a broad knowledge of the topic to make alterations in your topic to accommodate the questions posed. Have someone make a list of questions asked on a chalkboard, butcher paper, or some other way to keep them handy for people to refer to during your presentation. Allowing questions in the beginning is not something that is recommended for first time or inexperienced presenters.

During

Questions during the meeting are better for small, informal groups. You may say that they can feel free to ask questions during your presentation. This is a great way to keep the group involved in the presentation, but questions can get out of hand. You may need to halt them to present your prepared information. Watch attendees for confused expressions. At some point, delay remaining questions until after the presentation.

After

The most common time to answer questions is at the end of the presentation to avoid interruptions. At this point, the attendees can ask more informed questions. Your presentation should have answered many of their questions and limit the number that need to be addressed at the end. Announce that you are finished and ask for questions. The facilitator should field and buffer the questions and let you answer them.

Show It to Me

The 3M Corporation reports that people only retain 10 percent of what they hear and 20 percent of what they see. However, when they see and hear the information, the retention level increases to 50 percent. For this reason, it is good to have visual aids with your presentation. Here are some other benefits to using graphic aids:

- They will reinforce your presentation.

- Visual aids shift the focus off you to keep attendees' attention.

- The effort you devote to creating visual aids gives you a better grasp of details.

- A detailed graphic or visual presentation helps your attendees understand that you have a thorough knowledge of the topic.

- Visual aids can be used as additional notes for your presentation, especially true with transparencies and PowerPoint presentations that contain your notes.

Simple visual aids are effective. Overly detailed graphics can detract from your presentation, so keep it easy to understand.

There are easy ways to keep your visual aids simple.

- Make sure that everyone can read them without problems. The type of visual aid you use will be determined by the number of people in the meeting and sometimes the size of the room.

- Keep the items simple and precise. It is better to stay on the topic and only include specific details that pertain to your presentation. Do NOT give too much information. It is good to only include four or five key points per page.

- Add some variety and color to keep your attendees' attention. Find an effective way to point to your visual aids as you speak.

- Do not stand still while you are talking. A little movement will keep people interested and keep your legs from going to sleep.

The topic and the number of attendees will help you decide which visual aids are the best options for your presentation. Make sure the items are big enough to be seen but small enough that you can manage. If you require special equipment, be sure it is available.

Games for More Effective Presentations

Snappy Summary

Why Play – Show attendees quick ways to summarize the key points of a presentation.

Materials – You need something to write on that the group can see: chalkboard, flip chart.

How to Play –

- Before you take a break, summarize what has been discussed and decided up to that point. Have attendees help you review the key points.

- It is good to keep going until you have at least 10 points. This is not a time to dwell on the points or ask questions. Just ask for people to remind the group of individual points. Say, "Thank you" and move on.

Questions for Your Group –

- Were you surprised by the information the group generated?
- If not, why weren't you surprised?
- Is there a way to increase the amount of information?
- Why is it good to hear what others feel are the important points?
- Look at the compiled list. How does it differ from your list?

Teambuilding

It is critical for your group to build a team atmosphere so that they work together and to accomplish more.

Games to Build a Team Atmosphere

The following exercises will teach your attendees to work as a team. Pick ones that you feel will work with your group. You really cannot overestimate the value of a group working as a team.

What Is on a Penny?

Why Play – This game demonstrates the importance of working together as a team and that each person has something to contribute to the project.

What You Need – A handout that shows both sides of a coin and another handout that only contains two circles on one of which you write "Front of a Penny" and on the other, "Back of a Penny." It would be good to enlarge the picture to make it easier to see the details. (You can use a handout that lists the features of a penny and have the group label where these are located.)

How to Play –

- Have each person take a few minutes to list each feature of a penny from memory.
- You can have each person list how many things they got correct.

- Have the attendees work together with their lists and give them a few minutes to see if they found everything.

- Recalculate and find how many items each team got correct.

- The differences illustrate what can be accomplished by working as a team.

Things to Consider –

- Did attendees realize how they miss the individual elements of things that they see each day?

- Are there ways to improve the details that we notice each day?

- How are attendees and their jobs affected by missing little details?

The Answer –

Front

- "In God We Trust"
- "Liberty"
- Date
- Mint Mark
- President Lincoln's portrait, facing right

Back

- "United States of America"
- "One Cent"
- "E Pluribus Unum"
- Lincoln Memorial
- 12 columns on the memorial
- Statue of Lincoln in the center of the columns

Basic Details

- Copper color
- Raised edge around the penny

- Front and back are inverted when compared with each other
- ¾ inch diameter
- ¹⁄₁₆ inch thick
- ⅙ oz – weight
- Rim is smooth on the outside

What is Your Claim to Fame?

Why Play – This activity encourages attendees to share person information with each other. It also helps your attendees get used to sharing and being aware of additional details about each other.

How to Play –

- Decide on one provocative question that you will ask at each meeting. You can include the question on the agenda that you circulate or tell the attendees what it is at the meeting. Each participant needs to write an answer in 20-30 words.

- Have each attendee tell the group their answer.

Some sample questions could include:

- Tell us about your greatest accomplishment. Is it personal or business?
- What possession do you treasure the most?
- What message would you like on a T-shirt?
- Whom do you admire the most? Why?
- What is the best book you ever read? Why is it the best?
- Tell us about your dream vacation.
- Tell us about the happiest day in your life.
- Tell us about the most fun you ever had.

Questions to Ask –

- What are the benefits of sharing private thoughts?
- Is it good to discuss personal hopes and dreams?

Traits of a Leader

Why Play – This activity helps the traits and qualities a leader needs.

What You Need – paper, pen, and pencil

How to Play –

- Compare the traits of a leader now as compared to ten years ago.
- Compare management styles now as compared to ten years ago.
- Have the attendees list five people who they consider to be leaders. Why do they see these people as leaders? (Avoid politics and religion.)
- Divide the attendees into groups and have them compare lists and discuss why they included the different people.

Questions to Ask

- Were the same type of people mentioned more often?
- Is there a reason these people were included?
- Were people such as teacher, parent, grandparent, coach named frequently?
- Who would they have included five or ten years ago?

10

OTHER MEETING ATTENDEES

Effective meeting leaders need to learn more about the individual members and the members as a group. Various members may have additional responsibilities at meetings. These duties will be discussed in this chapter along with responsibilities of the participants. There may be times when your group needs a speaker and we will discuss ways to find a speaker and how to integrate their talks into your meeting plans.

KNOW YOUR GROUP

Each group of people has its own dynamic. An effective meeting leader needs to analyze and evaluate this dynamic. Are there things that need to be changed? Are there things that can be used for the good of the group? These are just a couple of the things for a meeting leader to consider and act upon.

Here is information that has an impact on the group and will shape the dynamics.

- Group History
- Sub Groups of the Main Group
- Individual Members and How They Affect the Group

- Group Membership as They Work Together
- Size of the Group
- Whether the Meetings Should be Formal or Informal

Meeting facilitators do not need to know the in depth history of the group and each member. In some cases this much knowledge could be harmful to the facilitator and the group as a whole. It is beneficial to know the basic history of the group and general information about each member. The facilitator should know the individual specialties of each members. This allows attendees to offer their best to the group.

The facilitator needs to learn the group dynamics—how the group members work together, what meeting design and plan is best for the group, and how to look at the group with fresh eyes.

Tricks to Learn New Names

The meeting leader and facilitator need to learn everyone's names because people appreciate being called on by name. These tips will also help other participants learn all members' names.

Name Linking – Have the first person say their name. The second person says their name and the previous name. The third person says their name and the previous two names. Use this technique to work your way around the room. An alternative is to let each person pick an adjective that begins with the same letter as their first name. This can make it easier to remember and make it more fun. A couple of examples include: Daring Dennis, Crazy Chris, Mighty Megan.

Take Time – Allow five or ten minutes for all attendees to learn as many names as possible. They can read name tags and introduce themselves. Have everyone remove their name tags and then pick specific attendees to name others around the room. The leader or facilitator should choose whom they will identify. Continue as long as you feel is needed.

Name Bingo – Give each attendee a blank bingo page. Mark the middle square as a free space. Attendees should mingle and write the names of other attendees in any blank. When the blocks are filled in, put each name on a piece of paper and draw these out one at a time and call out the names. Each attendee marks the names as they are called, just like a bingo game. When anyone has all blocks in a row, that person wins.

Name Tag Tag – Hand out name tags to the wrong people and have them find the owner.

It is All in a Name – Let each attendee say his or her own name and share something personal about their name. These can include: what they like about the name, what they dislike about the name, a nickname they like, a nickname they dislike, the origin of their name, and who they were named after. When everyone has taken a turn, have attendees write down the names of each meeting participant.

Factors That Affect the Group's Dynamic

External elements can include the expectations of the group. What do they expect to be normal? Consider their beliefs and assumptions. It is important to evaluate thoughts of the public, employees, supervisors, customers, and vendor. The facilitator needs to acknowledge and discuss the impact of these external elements. Ground rules for the group may need to be adjusted to suit the group more effectively.

The group history is something that everyone should be open and honest about. Whether the history is good or bad, it has a definite impact on the dynamics of the group. This history will include past problems that have been overcome and problems that the group may continue to work on. Some issues will mold the group's activities. The facilitator and leader need to help the group move past these problems. There are also elements of the group's history that will be positive. It is good to note these things when appropriate.

The history of individual attendees can have some impact on the group. It is only important if it helps or hinders the group in some way. Be honest about the positive and negative effects of past members and leaders. Once it is addressed and handled, everyone needs to agree to put it behind them. This is the best course of action for the group as a whole.

The group size has an impact on how the group should be handled. One initial decision is whether to conduct formal or informal meetings. Formal facilitation is recommended for larger groups. However, smaller groups can be handled in an informal manner and usually the members can monitor their own behavior. The facilitator or leader should not hesitate to step in and take the necessary action when problems arise. It is helpful for any facilitator or leader to be honest with themselves and others about their comfort level with small and large groups. This will help you prepare meetings that are the most effective.

Members of the group need to work well with each other, integrating new members easily. Keep an eye open for members who are quiet. Everyone needs to participate and contribute to the group and they need to understand the group's ground rules. At times you may find it useful to break the group into subgroups. This can be an effective strategy. However, it is good to have the members of these subgroups speak and interact with people from other subgroups. Do not let them forget that they are part of a larger group and need to work together.

Group leaders need to understand the difference between formal and informal leadership. This leadership should be evaluated to ensure no one is leading the group into a negative direction. It is up to the group members to keep the group on track. This means that any situation that could be detrimental to the group should be handled right away.

ATTENDEE RESPONSIBILITIES

Participation is a duty of every member. The amount of participation needed may vary, but each person has been included because the information, experience, or knowledge they bring to the group. For the group members to benefit from these things, the person must participate.

Are You a Good Participant

Let us discuss your participants' responsibilities.

- Arrive on time and stay until the end, longer if needed.

- Ask your questions and state your thoughts in a tactful manner.

- Support the meeting leader when useful suggestions are mentioned.

- Avoid unnecessary side conversations during the meeting.

- Draw conclusions about suggestions based on their merit, not by the person who made the suggestion or the way they presented the information.

- Pay attention and really listen to what is being said.

- Do not make rushed decisions about an idea until you hear the details.

- Make notes in a way that you can refer to them in the future.

- Work to block out distractions and focus on the meeting's purpose.

If you would like to create handouts to help your participants learn how to be more effective, the examples below would be a good start. The first outlines the qualities of a good participant and the second helps each person evaluate their contribution to the meeting.

Qualities of a Good Meeting Participant
Do You Have These Qualities?

Prepare for the meeting before it begins.

Offer suggestions and ideas about issues or problems being discussed.

Do your best to keep the meeting orderly.

Follow through on the decisions.

Listen when others offer suggestions and ideas.

Consider the ideas in an objective manner.

Give appropriate and constructive feedback to the meeting leader.

For meeting attendees who would like to evaluate their participation, this form will help them see if there are ways they can improve.

YOUR MEETING PARTICIPATION CHECKLIST		
Check yes or no concerning your performance.	YES	NO
1. Do I know the purpose for each meeting I attend before it begins?		
2. Do I confirm with the leader that I will be at the meeting?		
3. Do I get to the meeting location before the meeting starts?		
4. Do I understand my role in each meeting I attend?		
5. Do I fully prepare for the meeting and complete any tasks assigned to me?		
6. Do I avoid all unnecessary "side conversations" during the meeting?		
7. Do I avoid any unnecessary distractions or reasons to leave the meeting?		
8. Do I listen to each point being discussed?		
9. Do I ask questions when I do not fully understand things being discussed?		
10. Do I remain open minded about new ideas?		
11. Do I encourage others to stay focused on the topic being discussed?		
12. Do I contribute to the discussions in a positive way?		
13. Do I follow-up on decisions that were made?		
14. Do I share relevant information with people who missed the meeting?		
15. Do I contribute useful feedback to the leader on ways to improve?		

How do your participants rate on the questions above? Each of the items listed above are ways to make your participants more effective and will help make your meetings more successful.

Behavior That Benefits the Group

This type of behavior encourages the group to accomplish goals and promotes a "group mentality."

Behavior When Working on Tasks

- Contribute and initiate ideas
- Summarize information that has been offered
- Ask questions before making final decisions
- Evaluate whether the group is ready to make decisions
- Do what is needed to clarify problems and concerns
- Seek out and provide additional details and information

Behavior When Developing Relationships

- Offer encouragement to other members
- Work to resolve conflicts in the group
- Offer constructive criticism and positive feedback
- Be friendly and cooperative with members in the group
- Encourage people to participate and include everyone in proceedings

Behavior that is for the Benefit of Individual Members

Conversely, there is behavior that only benefits one individual and will damage the group, discouraging a "group mentality."

- Arriving late for meetings and leaving early
- Offering negative asides about everyone's comments
- Keeping important information to themselves
- Trying to take over the meeting to the exclusion of others
- Seeming to agree, but then adding a "but."
- Refusing to participate in a positive and helpful manner

- Refusing to acknowledge the group's efforts
- Belittling others and making negative comments about their efforts
- Holding private discussions during the meeting
- Diminishing the efforts of group members

Roles Within the Meeting

These are some of the roles your participants may assume, all of which are not necessary. Some of the last roles are only used in specific meeting situations. I am including all details for the situations where you need any of these people in your meeting.

Facilitator

The facilitator helps plan the agenda and leads the meeting. It is not up to the facilitator to contribute any thoughts about the agenda topics as this person needs to remain neutral and keep the meeting focused and on track. The leader creates the structure and direction for the meeting. This person also encourages participation and guides problem solving.

Leader

The leader calls the meeting based on a specific need. This can be the need to find a solution to a problem, to make a decision, or to disseminate information to the group. The leader will often choose the others within the group who will manage the other duties or may ask for qualified volunteers.

Recorder or Minutes Taker

This person records the information shared in the meeting. It is acceptable for other members of the group to mention information the recorder missed in his or her summary. However, it is better to wait until the meeting is over to mention these details. After the meeting is over, this information needs to be used to create the minutes for the meeting and distribute to all people who need a copy, including attendees.

Record Keeper

This person maintains all records for the meeting: agenda, minutes, attendee information, reports, handouts, correspondence, and data.

Timekeeper

This person keeps track of the timing for the meeting and notifies the speaker, facilitator, or other people about how much time remains for each segment of the meeting.

Flip Chart Keeper

This is the person responsible to keep all ideas on a flip chart. They can transport the flip chart to and from each meeting along with writing implements. It is good to pick a person with good handwriting who is organized and listens well.

Meeting Planner

You may have a person who coordinates and organizes the meeting location, set up, invitations, food, and other miscellany.

Researcher

One person can be assigned to do all research for the topics the group will discuss. This can help you avoid wasted time because multiple people are researching the same information.

Participants

The meeting participants need to contribute ideas, suggestions, thoughts, and additional information to help the group make an educated and informed decision.

FEATURE ATTENDEES

There are different sorts of people you can feature including speakers, debaters, trainers, and commentators. The first group we will talk about are speakers. Meeting speakers can be big name celebrities or they can be an expert in a specific field. The type of speaker you invite can depend on your needs, your budget, and your goals. It is not necessary to have a celebrity speak. In every community, there are local experts in their field. These people are able to provide insights into your topic and provide relevant information to your attendees.

Some places to find speakers within your area include:

- **Social Services** – health, social concerns, family topics

- **Local Hospitals** – health and possibly business topics

- **Health Department** – health issues

- **Non-Profit Organizations** – contacts with many local businesses

- **United Way** – contacts with many local business people

- **Local Industries** – business people on many various topics, public relations, human resources, many possibilities

- **Chamber of Commerce** – contact with local business people and local government representatives on a broad variety of subjects

- **Local Government** – city manager, city planner, mayor county administrators, county board of supervisor, and other local officials

- **Local School System** – school superintendent and other school board members can speak on a variety of topics

- **Local Colleges, Universities, and Community Colleges** – Great source for speakers on many different topics and business resources

These are just some of the local possibilities. Once you begin meeting other business people, network with them to find out about other people and possibilities.

Bringing in Speakers from Outside

There may be some times when you need an outside speaker. Obtaining one can be a simple process or can be involved depending on the meeting and the type of speaker you want. Keep in mind the bigger name person, the more money and complications there will be. We will discuss basic principles of scheduling speakers and I will include some details about high profile speakers.

Some of the types of speakers are:

- Motivational speakers

- Specialists in a particular relevant field or topic

- Outside experts who can teach your attendees more about a relevant topic

There are many places to find speakers. Some of the larger resources include; Speakers Bureaus and National Speaks Association along with other resources listed later in this chapter with their Web site addresses.

Locally, I would begin with the Chamber of Commerce. It is amazing how much information the staff of your Chamber of Commerce has at their disposal. Some other local resources could include:

- Local colleges

- Local politicians in all levels of government – mayor, city council, and board of supervisors

- Local attorneys, doctors, business owners, or business and community leaders

- Notable individuals in the community such as prominent business people. Who is consistently in the news? Could get information from local newspaper office, chamber of commerce, or local clubs and organizations. These are just a few. What organizations and clubs are in your area?

  o Boy Scouts and Girl Scouts

  o Country Club

  o Eagles

- o Ruritan Club
- o Lion's Club
- o BNI – Business Networking International

The Internet makes it easier than ever to find experts in various fields. However, if you find a Web site where a person claims to be an expert, be sure to check them out and insist on getting references. Anyone can create a Web site and say they are an expert, but you need to make sure they know what they are talking about and that they are right for your meeting needs.

Speakers Bureau

The Speakers Bureau handles all contracts, travel arrangements, equipment needs, and most details for the speaker. They can help you choose the right speaker for your meeting. Many times they have taped samples of speeches for you to review. Do not hesitate to tell the people at the Speakers Bureau if you feel they have suggested the wrong person for your group. Insist on references whom you can call—and then call them. Ask questions and listen carefully to their response. It is great to be able to talk with the speaker before your meeting. I also recommend that you have a qualified person review any contract before you sign.

National Speakers Association

There are 3,800 speakers associated with the National Speakers Association chapters.

The chapter directory can be found at the link below. You can find a speaker based on location, topic, name, and budget to give you the chance to deal with the speaker directly. (**http://www.nsaspeaker.org/search/chapter-directory.xpl**)

Are You Ready to Hire?

Once you take a look at available speakers, you need to make a final decision. Keep in mind that it is important to hire the right speaker for your meeting. Do not feel pressured to choose someone who is not right for you. This applies to local individuals or professional speakers. Just because the person is a speaker, that does not mean they are right for you.

Here are some tips to consider when you hire a speaker.

- Get information about the potential speaker, their background, and expertise. You need to talk with the speaker before your event or meeting. It is helpful to see their speech outlines to give you an idea of the content and their approach to the topic.

- It is helpful to review videotapes or audio tapes of their previous speeches. This will help you to get a better idea of the speaker's style.

- You need to request a list of references from the speaker and check them. Call the individuals and find out what the speaker's subject was. Ask if they were happy and for details if they were not. It is good to ask if there were problems before you make a final decision.

- Talk to the speaker personally. Can you communicate with each other? If not, this may not be the person for your meeting. Ask questions about the topic to ensure the speaker does know the subject. Discuss how you plan to integrate their talk into your agenda. All details need to be discussed and resolved before the meeting and preferably before signing a contract.

- Confirm any travel, lodging, food, and other expenses that your company would be responsible to pay since they may be high. Even with local speakers, you may be expected to pay for their gas or transportation and possible a meal or two. Out-of-town speakers could insist on first-class travel and may not be flexible about a travel day. Each of these items will raise your costs substantially.

- Determine any audio or video needs. What will you need to supply for their presentation? The speaker may expect things that you or the facility does not offer. This can include: particular podium, special microphone, overhead projector, special screens, unusual or expensive sound and lighting equipment.

- Verify all fees—including any hidden fees.

- Always have a backup plan and especially when you are dealing with a new person. Unforeseen things happen, so it is always advisable to have a "Plan B."

Communication with the speaker is important. This can be any sort of communication, including phone, fax, or e-mail. I personally like to speak to someone on the phone before they arrive at an event that I plan. One important thing that you need to discuss is the contract or letter of agreement. These items should include the following information.

- Date, time, length of talk, and specific location for speech.

- Detail any travel arrangements.

- List the topic or title of the speech to be given. If you want to make alterations to an existing speech, list any changes to avoid confusion.

- Outline all fees and note that it is a complete list.

- Outline any handouts, equipment, or other special things that you need to supply, including equipment, number of copies, flip charts, markers, and any other items the speaker needs you to supply.

- Request an advance copy of the speech. This is a personal preference but something for you to consider.

- In situations where other people will be included in the presentation, you can ask to speak to them in advance and inquire about their qualifications.

- Explain the size and setup of the room to the speaker. If the speaker has any requests for room layout, discuss these in advance and resolve before signing the contract.

- Give the speaker an outline of break times along with the beginning and ending time for the speech and the meeting.

On the day of the meeting, be at the meeting site early to allow time to verify everything is ready, You can also greet the speaker and possibly introduce him or her to meeting attendees. The meeting leader or facilitator needs to be prepared to introduce the speaker. Verify the specific information to be sure the speaker's introduction is correct.

Points to Consider About Meeting Speakers

Know the Message for Your Meeting

- What is the message you plan to get across in this meeting?
- How will you structure the meeting to communicate this message?
- Will the outside speaker fit into your agenda?
- What is the reason for having the speaker: lighten the mood, act as an emcee, additional training for the attendees?
- How important is the outside speaker to the success of the meeting?
- What kind of speaker will help you meet your goal for the meeting (celebrity, sports figure, industry expert, etc.)?
- At what point in the meeting should the speaker begin?
- What do you want attendees to take away from the speaker's presentation?

Tap Into Your Experience

- Who is the best speaker you ever had? Why?
- Who was the worst speaker you've had? Why?
- How would your meeting be affected if the speaker were not available?
- Did the speaker have the desired impact?
- Did the speaker meet your expectations?
- How much did the speaker add to the meeting?
- Did the speaker contribute to the theme of your meeting?
- How did attendees respond to the presentation?

- Compile your thoughts about the speaker and share them with your representative at the Speaker's Bureau. These notes will be a big help the next time you work together.

Online Speaker Resources

Here are some online resources to find speakers for your meeting. There is a wealth of information on their sites about meeting planning and finding the right speaker. Keep in mind that many will include fees. Be sure that you understand all fees to be incurred.

Association of Job Search Trainers
http://www.ajst.org/HTML/findaspeaker.asp

Find a Speaker
www.find-speaker.com

National Speakers Association
www.nsaspeaker.org / 3,800 speakers

Online Continuing Education Resource
www.findce.com

Resource for Celebrity Speakers
www.lectureagent.com

Speaker Match – Request the Speaker You Want
www.speakermatch.com/orgs.asp

Toastmasters
www.toastmasters.org

Walters International Speakers Bureau
www.walters-intl.com

Women's Resource Center Speaker Information
http://www.womenscenter.gatech.edu/speakersbureau.html

CASE STUDY

One of the first things I did when I signed a publishing contract for my first book was to join Toastmasters International. My goal was simple. When my book made it to print, I was going to need to promote it. That meant book-signings and speeches—both of which terrified me. I'd heard many good things about Toastmasters and figured it was a great way to learn how to prepare and deliver a presentation and to handle impromptu questions without passing out or creating annoying background noise from my knees knocking.

Over the course of the next few months I learned that Toastmasters is about more than giving speeches. The club mission statement says it all. "The mission of a Toastmasters Club is to provide a mutually supportive and positive learning environment in which every member has the opportunity to develop communication and leadership skills, which in turn foster self-confidence and personal growth."

An interesting thing about Toastmasters is the way in which the meetings are conducted. As a member you'll take turns volunteering to serve any one of a number of different functions at each meeting. Sometimes it will be that of Toastmaster for the day, which means you'll develop the agenda and conduct the meeting. Other times it might be moderating Table Topics (impromptu two-minute speeches), evaluating a speaker or the meeting in general, or giving a speech. No matter what function you serve at a given meeting, the opportunities to sharpen speaking, listening, and leadership skills is always front and center.

Did Toastmasters help me to achieve my goals? Absolutely. Recently, I launched a lecture series based on my book *Retire Rich With Your Self-Directed IRA*. What surprises me most is how much I enjoy doing it now that I am confident in my ability to control both my nerves and the flow of the meeting.

For more information about Toastmasters International or to find a club near you, visit their Web site at **www.toastmasters.org**.

Nora Peterson, stock trader, novelist, and nonfiction author

Author of *Retire Rich with Your Self-Directed IRA: What Your Broker and Banker Do Not Want You to Know About Managing Your Own Retirement Investments* and *Wall Street Lingo.*

Ms. Peterson has been involved in the financial markets for more than thirty years. She is the author of *Retire Rich with Your Self-Directed IRA: What Your Broker and Banker Do not Want You to Know About Managing Your Own Retirement Investment* and *Wall Street Lingo,* a finance dictionary for Main Street investors. For more information about Nora's work, visit her at **www.norapeterson.com.**

11

COMMUNICATION

———

Communication is critical in any situation and especially important in business. Meetings are about conveying information or solving problems through effective communication among the meeting participants. Some of the ways people communicate include listening, speaking, stating thoughts and opinions, giving a report, posing questions, offering answers, and working through problems and concerns.

It is important to set the right tone for your meetings. The leader or facilitator needs to be sure the meeting room is ready before the meeting begins. This includes completing the following meeting preparations.

- **Room Setup** – chair and table setup, check ventilation, and temperature

- **Visual Aids** – Flip charts, handouts, transparencies, posters

The leader should also be available to greet attendees as they arrive. Taking a moment to say hello, call them by name, and mention something to them personally are great ways to get things started on a good footing with the attendees. You give them a chance to get to know you personally so they will open up and participate. A positive tone for your meeting is important. Even if a negative or troublesome topic is being discussed, keep the meeting positive. Gauge the tone of the attendees and determine what sort of attitude is needed to be the most effective with the participants.

LISTEN

Listening is a big part of communication. Effective meeting leaders and attendees need to learn how to listen. Let us discuss ways to improve your listening abilities. There are verbal and nonverbal listening skills and both of these are important for effective facilitation. Remember that both techniques have their place in your meetings.

Verbal Listening

Verbal listening skills include reviewing the information that has been shared with the group. This can include summarizing details the speaker or other attendees said to the meeting attendees. These are listening skills to help you be a better, more effective leader or facilitator. When someone says they are tired of the way things are, these are a few ways you can reply.

- "So, you are tired of the way the meeting is run?"

- "Are you saying that you want to recommend some changes?"

- "You sound irritated and unhappy with our meeting."

- "Will you tell me what you do not like about our meeting?"

Each reply accomplishes something different and the one you use depends on the person you are talking with and what you need to accomplish with them.

Nonverbal Listening

Nonverbal listening includes a different set of skills:

Body Position – The most accepted positions to convey equality include sitting on the edge if a table or chair or standing. Maintain a relaxed position for equal feelings. Never crowd the person or get "in their face."

Eye Contact – It is good to maintain eye contact 70 percent to 80 percent of the time based on local or native eye contact behavior.

Facial Expressions – Your facial expressions can and usually will affect the person you are listening to. Do not yawn, look bored, roll your eyes, or perform similar actions that are disrespectful. It is even important to smile at the right times. Remember that your face reveals a lot about what you are thinking and feeling.

Silence – People need time to express themselves and many times they need the person to just stay quiet for a few minutes. Give them time to form the words to get their point across to you and the other attendees.

DO NOT DISCOURAGE PARTICIPATION

Let us start by listing some things that discourage participation. These are some things that attendees find frustrating and discouraging.

- No prepared agenda
- A leader who is obviously unprepared
- Too many side points being discussed
- No real focus
- Only a few people have a chance to participate
- They may feel unqualified to participate
- They may be cut off when they try to share
- Topics may be carried over from one meeting to the next
- Attendees are not given the information and time to prepare
- There is no summary to ensure everyone understands decisions

Some solutions to these problems are knowing the people in your meeting, choosing the best people for the topics to be discussed, being prepared, and allowing attendees to have a chance to prepare.

Diversity is important. Did you invite a group of people that represents all sides of an issue? It is crucial to be able to view an issue from all angles and to ensure the topic is thoroughly discussed. Never pick the first people who come to mind. Instead, think about the people who are available and find specific ones who will contribute the most to the meeting and the topics to be discussed.

ENCOURAGE PARTICIPATION

Meeting leaders and facilitators need to encourage participation. Above we discussed things you should avoid since they discourage participation. On the other hand this section offers tips and suggestions to encourage your attendees to participate more fully in your meetings.

Tips to Encourage Participation

Here are some techniques that could work with your group.

- **Open the Floor for Comments** – This is the easiest and usually generates the most participation. You can ask the attendees if they have any thoughts or comments. Limit the number of comments to be taken, but get things moving and bring people into the discussion.

- **Choose or Assign Partners** – Attendees can be divided into pairs or small groups and assigned specific activities, a good way to ease hesitant people into discussions and break the ice with large groups.

- **Index Cards** – You can use three-by-five inch index cards for attendees to write their responses to your questions to ease them into participating and allow them to give anonymous suggestions for more controversial topics. You would not want to do this with every question or topic, but it could be a good answer for some situations.

- **Panel Discussion** – Select several attendees to form a panel and possibly sit at the front of the room. They can be chosen to offer their thoughts about a topic that coordinates with the agenda. You must let the people know that they were chosen before the meeting so they can be prepared.

Meeting Packets

This is a unique idea that helps build participant excitement. Prepare and distribute meeting packets filled with information to make the meeting feel like an event. A prepared packet gives the attendees details about the meeting and shows them that you are prepared and want them to be prepared. The detail or size of the packet is determined by the size of the meeting and the amount of detail in your agenda.

Here are some tips and suggestions to make your meeting packets interesting.

- Choose a nice folder. You can have them printed with your company logo or buy a nice "crack and peel" sticker to place on the cover.

- Place a pencil or reasonably priced pen in the folder to encourage writing notes.

- Include a copy of the meeting agenda, a list of the attendees, a seating plane, reference materials that apply to the agenda, and a list of Web site addresses for related research. You may include recent data, budget details, letters, or any other print information which is useful for the meeting.

- Blank sheets of paper or lined paper can be included for taking note. You can easily create a sheet of paper or a form corresponding to the agenda, leaving room for attendee notes.

- If you have problems with specific behavior or ground rules, it can be good to include a sheet with reminders about these items. It is a courtesy to those who abide by the rules.

- Some people like to add stress reduction tips or energy boosters, simple exercises that can be done at your chair to relieve stress along with back and neck stiffness. Or this could be any health tip that would be helpful for attendees.

- If you are meeting in an unusual location, include location details to help your attendees find the meeting easier with floor plan, room location. location of restrooms, water fountains, drink and snack machines, elevators, escalators, stairways and emergency exits, parking areas, and any specific instructions, with special information for people with disabilities marked clearly.

INTERACTION

One thing that will prompt interaction with your attendees is to give them information before the meeting and assign research or preparation duties to each one. The better they prepare, the more likely they will participate and the more effective your meeting can be. A part of your meeting planning needs to include a list of the things the attendees need to do in preparation for the meeting.

Review your agenda and determine what attendees need to do to be fully prepared for the meeting. What do they need to do to contribute to a productive meeting?

- Some attendees can do some assigned reading. Each attendee may read the same information, or you can assign different reading assignments and then each person can summarize the information during the meeting.

- When all attendees read the same material, have each person look for a different type of information. This will allow your group to look at the information from various perspectives and fully evaluate the details.

- Are there people who have information that would be beneficial for your group? Why not assign certain members to interview them? These members can then share the information with the group. This can be especially helpful when there are experts who cannot attend your meetings, but you would still like to share their knowledge with the attendees.

- A similar idea is to assign specific research to various members of your group. This can be any information that would coordinate with your agenda topic and would be beneficial for your meeting attendees.

- Some attendees can be assigned to do a simple survey or an experiment to attain information for the group.

CASE STUDY

Weekly sales meetings are a communication tool in my office when everyone gets together. The meetings set the tone in the office for the rest of the week. They must be topical, informative, upbeat, and short. To get my associates to listen to me, I let them know that I am open to listening to them. At the end of every meeting I conduct a debriefing of what is going on in our sales market. I do moderate the discussion to keep the meeting on track and on time, but my associates are free to discuss what they want and I do listen. Sometimes the material for the next sales meeting comes out of these candid discussions.

Every now and then, I need to get my associates out of the office to break the monotony of the weekly sales meeting. Off-site meetings are planned in advance and they have a specific purpose. One of my off-site meetings entail getting a promotional picture of our staff for Thanksgiving and Christmas. In the fall, the leaves in Virginia's Shenandoah Valley are beautiful. We took a picture of all our associates on an overlook on the Blue Ridge Parkway. We asked everyone to wear a sweater or sweatshirt with the company logo for the picture. The multi-colored leaves in the background made for a sensational seasonal marketing piece.

Unplanned off-site sales meetings also are effective. Periodically, I will have a sales meeting at a local restaurant for breakfast or at a local coffee house. The associates in my company show up for the usual sales meeting, and I announce that there is not sales meeting, but that instead, I will take everyone out to coffee or breakfast. We then pile in our cars and take it on the road. This type of meeting is strictly informal and without an agenda. My associates seem to take great relief in the meeting being "cancelled," but almost everyone shows up for the free coffee. What these "meetings" have allowed is complete comfort. This style of meeting makes for relaxed discussion. It is hard for an associate to be tense while sipping a latte and sitting on a deeply cushioned couch.

My associates are used to a meeting that starts on time, has an agenda, and ends on time. With such a structure they stay informed and keep me informed about what is going on in the trenches. The occasional unstructured meeting has become a real treat that is good for morale. It also gives my associates a chance to share what is in their hearts and not just what is on their minds.

Kevin S. Sweeney GRI, ABR

* 1994 Leader of 200 by 2000 Leadership Training Institute Steering Committee

* 1997–2005 Winner of Greater Augusta County and Staunton Augusta Association of REALTORS President's Award of Excellence

* 2002 REALTOR of the Year for the Greater Augusta Association of REALTORS

* 2004 President of the Staunton Augusta Association of REALTORS

* Currently the Managing Broker of RE/MAX Advantage in Waynesboro, VA and Manager of Home Front Title and Settlement

This may seem obvious, but tell your attendees that you want them to prepare for meetings. There are meeting leaders who do not care whether attendees prepare. When attendees find useful information, it is good for them to forward the details to you. A simple summary can keep you informed without wasting time reading all the information. E-mail is a great way to send this information to you. Otherwise, they can call or fax you about the details.

DISCUSSIONS

This is a simple principle that all meeting leaders and participants need to understand. The leader needs to create an atmosphere where attendees feel free to share their thoughts and ideas about the topics being discussed without retribution. Good questioning skills help the meeting draw more information from the attendees.

Here are some tips to help you generate discussion in your meetings. Keep your ears open for cues about potential problems and questions. When your attendees fidget, scribble on their paper, and their eyes glaze over in boredom your meeting is in trouble.

We will discuss questioning in more detail in the next section. Here are several types of questions to get a discussion started.

- **Direct** – Ask one or two specific people.

- **General** – Ask many people and request a broad range of answers.

- **Specific** – Focus attendees on a limited topic.

General questions are perceived as less threatening, while direct and specific questions put more pressure on individuals. In the beginning, it may be important to think carefully about whom you ask the direct and specific questions.

Here are some examples of things to consider when you are working to generate discussion in your meeting.

1. **Feelings** – Ask questions that encourage people to share what they feel.

   - What are your feelings about...?

   - What is your reaction...?

   - How did you arrive at that do you think about...?

   - How could we...?

2. **Encourage** – There are times when people do not want to share their thoughts and you need to encourage them to participate.

You can address questions to a specific person. As mentioned above, be careful who you "put on the spot."

- George, how do you feel about that?

- Helen, what do you think about that?

- After the break, let us hear what Elaine thinks.

3. **Help your participants get to the point** – Sometimes you need to interrupt with, "Would you state that once more clearly?" When you prepare for the meeting, it is not a bad idea to note the questions you want to ask and include different ways to ask the questions. You may also need them to state their answers a different way. When you do not understand or if others look confused, do not be afraid to ask another question.

- "Did you mean...?

- "Do you want to know...?

- "Let me see if I understand what you mean."

- "I did not understand your question. Could you ask it again?"

4. **In Summary** – It is good to summarize. It gives you a chance to repeat the information that was generated and make sure nothing was missed.

- "Let us summarize the main points before we move to the next item on the agenda."

- "Would someone like to summarize the decisions we reached today?"

- "Would someone like to summarize the major problems they have with the discussion?"

5. **For Example** – It is good to illustrate the point you are trying to make.

- "Can anyone give us an example of how that would work?"

- "We might need a few more details so that everyone will understand."

6. **Let Us Get Started** – When a decision is made, it is time to proceed.

   - "Does anyone want to offer a suggestion on how to get started?"

   - "I would like some suggestions on the best way to proceed with this plan."

7. **Dig Deeper** – There are times when you do not have enough details to make an educated decision. In these instances, you need to dig for more information.

   - "Are there any suggestions on other ways to solve this problem?"

   - "What other possibilities should we consider?"

   - "I haven't heard anything about...."

These are just a few examples of ways to generate discussion and resolve some problems and issues in a variety of situations.

- If you want to stimulate conversation... ask the group a general question.

- If you want to stop conversation... ask one person to give the group a summary.

- To draw people into the discussion... ask a general question of one person.

- When two people have a side conversation... ask one of them a specific question.

- When you do not know the answer to a question... ask the group for their input.

- When you want to see how the group feels... ask a specific question of the group.

- When two attendees argue a point... ask one to summarize the discussion so far.

- When progress in a discussion is unclear... ask attendees to summarize the facts.

- When two people argue with no progress... ask each to sum up their thoughts.

- When you need to know if you are effective... ask attendees for their feedback.

FACILITATE DISCUSSIONS

Active meetings need plenty of discussion. This also requires a facilitator who knows how to handle, control, and encourage discussion. Here are some tips to facilitate discussion.

- **Say It Another Way** – Sometimes you simply need to state your question in a different way. The attendees may not understand your question, so it is good to prepare a set of questions instead of one. This will help you be prepared if you need to paraphrase your question or thoughts.

- **Keep it Positive** – When attendees make a suggestion or comment, find something positive to say in response. If something negative needs to be said, that should be said privately. In this situation, carefully word the positive comment that is made to the group.

- **What Did You Say** – Are you confused by a comment that was made? Maybe others are confused, too. Find a way to verify that you heard them correctly. One approach could be, "Do you mean that..." or "Can you explain that in some more detail?"

- **Tie Them Together** – There are times when attendees share ideas that can work together. Are there ways that you can combine ideas and comments to create a plan for the group? Stay open to these possibilities.

- **Broaden the Horizon** – You will find some ideas can be easily expanded for the group. When an attendee makes a suggestion, it could be useful to ask others for ideas on ways to expand the idea. This is a great way to brainstorm and make a good idea even better.

- **Keep it Civil** – If two attendees begin to argue, it is important to jump in before it gets out of hand. Let them talk a little while but step in before it gets bad. Remind them that they are seeing two different sides of the situation. This does not mean that one or the other is wrong, because there are multiple ways to see the same issue or problem. This is one of the reasons that meetings can be so effective. It gives various people a chance to share their opinions to help the group make an educated decision.

SKILLFUL QUESTIONING

Questions are an everyday part of a meeting leader's life. Attendees will come to you with questions. There are also times in your meeting when you need to ask appropriate questions to elicit information from participants. Ineffective questioning will result in loss of their respect and cooperation.

Learning to ask and answer questions properly is critical for effective leaders. There will be times when you need to ask questions. You may need details about the meeting topics. To get the details you want, you may need to ask different types of questions. We'll discuss the techniques to get the information you need.

Learn to Ask Questions—The Right Way

The way questions are asked will determine the type of answers you receive. For example, if you sound pleasant, attendees are likely to respond in a positive and helpful manner. Avoid tones or words that seem adversarial or confrontational.

Do you provide an atmosphere in your meetings that is conducive to honesty? Make it possible for your participants to give you honest answers without worrying about repercussions. Help them understand that a person can be honest without being rude.

These are some of the things you can learn through the use of skillfully asking questions.

- What do the various people or departments need?

- What can they contribute to the topic you are discussing or the problem you are trying to solve?

- What critical insights can they offer?

- How can you and your attendees accomplish more?

- What deeper insights can you discover which will help your attendees?

Effective leaders need to communicate with attendees effectively. Take time to discover what you want to know and use the tips shared in these pages to find a way to get those answers.

Think of it like planning a trip. You know where you want to end: At the answer to your question. Once the answer is clear in your mind, figure how you can get to that answer. If you begin that trek with no plan, you may wander around with useless questions before you reach the answer you and the group need.

Types of Questions

Some questions will clarify your point, while others expand your understanding of facts or issues. The questions you should use depend on what you want to learn. Do you need a simple answer or a more complicated and involved answer? The following explanations will help you understand how to phrase questions to draw out the answers you need.

- **Clarification and Confirmation** – Begin your questions with: "Can," "Do," "Is," "Will," "When," "Who," and "Did." These questions will lead to yes or no answers or other short answers. Use these questions when you do not need a lot of details. These are called "closed" questions.

- **Additional Clarification** – Begin these questions with "How," "What," and "Why." The answers to these questions need more detailed answers. They are called "open" questions because hey require more thought and effort, and they give you more information.

- **Expand the Response** – Answers to these questions let you dig deeper for details. Use these questions after you get partial answers to your other questions. Those initial answers will help you know what other information is needed.

When an attendee gives a partial answer, include a portion of their answer in your next question. This is a good approach when the first answer is too broad. You can narrow the focus when you repeating the portion of the answer that pertains to the information you need. It is important to follow-up on the answers you receive. If there are details that the employee left out or if you need to zero in on specific facts, ask more questions until you are satisfied.

One of the most important things is to remain positive when you ask questions. Even if you become frustrated, you need to keep an even tone and remain calm. You may be tempted to be sneaky or sarcastic with your employees, but that is a dead-end street.

A basic principle in communication is to maintain eye contact when you speak to anyone. This is especially true when you need information from a meeting attendee. Have you ever talked to someone who will not look you in the eye? Did you feel the person was hiding something? Your attendees will feel the same way if you avoid their eyes. Maintaining eye contact shows you care about them and are being honest with them. When you give them your attention, they will give you their attention in return.

When you ask a specific question, do attendees give you an unusual answer? Does their response confuse you? Perhaps your question was not worded well. If the question is confusing, the answer it elicits can reflects that. When this happens find another way to ask for the information you need.

The better your questions become, the more comfortable and responsive the meeting attendees should be with you. Make them feel comfortable and you should gain more useful information. They will hold back when they are uncomfortable.

Effective questioning is a skill that you will need to learn with practice. It is not natural for many people but with practice you can pose questions for the participants in your meeting to get the information you need. Sometimes you only need to approach the topic from a different perspective. These skills will help you work around and past vague answers. Over time you will build and improve your skills and you will be more effective.

There are times when it is tempting to cut people short when they are asking questions. This is especially true when a meeting is running late and the agenda is not being covered, but you should not cut people short in the meeting. If you need to wrap up questions at that point, address the entire group. This is important so that it does not look like you are chastising one person. Do whatever you can to help your attendees feel comfortable and confident meeting with you. You can accomplish this by focusing on their question and helping them as quickly as possible.

12

TOOLS FOR EFFECTIVE MEETINGS

There are many tools that can be used to make your meeting more interesting and to make the information more visual for the attendees. One method is through the use of games. A number of games have been included in the appropriate areas of the book. There are also different ways to gather information, organize this data, grouping and sequencing the information for the best possible presentation to your group.

GATHERING THE DATA

Here are some questions to consider to determine the best way to organize and gather the information you plan to use in your meeting.

- Do you have the information that you need?

- Is there enough information for a thorough presentation?

- Are all elements of the topic or subject represented in the information you have?

- Do you need additional people to help you collect more information?

ORGANIZING FOR BEST PRESENTATION

- Have you organized the information you plan to present?

- Can your group use the information the way you have it organized?

- Is further organization needed?

- If so, who should organize the information?

GROUPING AND SEQUENCING INFORMATION FOR THE GROUP

- Have your grouped and sequenced the information?

- Is that the best way to compile the data?

- Is grouping the best way to organize the details?

- Is there an obvious way to sequence the information?

- Can you determine steps, processes, levels, stages, and timelines for the data?

- Do additional people need to work with the grouping and sequencing projects?

MEETING GAMES

In various chapters of this book, I included games that you can use at your meetings. Some will help break the ice, some help the attendees learn to work together, and others will help you solve problems. Do not let games take up too much of your meeting time, but in some situations they are a good way to work with the attendees and possibly help participants get past some problems.

The games should not take the place of the meeting or the agenda. They are used in conjunction with the meeting and to improve your meetings.

Attendees want meetings that are fast paced, lively, innovative, participative, and imaginative. Do your meetings fit this description?

Some of the descriptions of games that help your meetings include

- **Fast** – Games may take five or ten seconds or five or ten minutes in most cases.

- **Inexpensive** – Games do not cost any money and use normal office supplies.

- **Chance to Participate** – Games encourage people to participate in activities.

- **Props** – Props may be needed for some games, but they are cheap and simple.

- **Low Risk** – When used in the right manner, these should not involve any risk.

- **Adaptability** – Most games can be adapted to your group and situation.

- **Single Focus** – Try to find games that relate to your meeting focus and needs.

Irrelevant and random games will not help your meeting or your attendees. However, if you follow these guidelines, it is possible to make your meetings more effective through the use of games.

- **Carefully Select Games** – Read this entire book and become familiar with all the games to help you make logical choices about which games to use in particular situations and for certain topics.

- **Talk with Other People** – Ask other meeting participants and leaders about games they may have used. It is beneficial to ask the following questions and additional questions that may come to you.

o   Did you use the game?

o   How did it work?

o   Did you find ways to make it more effective?

o   Have you found alternatives that worked for you?

o   Can I get more details?

- **Have a Plan** – Remember that things often go wrong, so have a back up plan. If you need props or handouts, have a plan in case there is a problem with these items.

- **A Practice Run** – Never use a game at your meeting without running through the details and trying it out with some people. Find a couple of people and play the game once or twice to make sure you understand the instructions and to see if you need to make any changes or adjustments.

Keep games in their proper place in your meeting. You should never use games just to entertain the attendees. Any games you use should have a definite purpose and the attendees should be able to understand the reason you are playing. It is important that you practice the games and be fully prepared before using any games at your meetings. They can be useful.

PREPARE DATA

The steps involved in preparing the data include gathering, organizing, grouping, sequencing, and breaking it down. We should discuss each of these elements in more detail.

Gather

There are many ways to gather information. Next, you will find more details on some of these methods.

Brainstorming

My favorite way to gather information is through brainstorming. Choose creative participants who understand the project. Let them evaluate, develop, and delete some possibilities. An open mind is a great way to enter a brainstorming session.

Brainstorming allows the group to get all ideas out in the open and to share thoughts about these ideas. Someone needs to be assigned to document all ideas that arise. Encourage everyone involved to be creative and open minded. It is important to keep the group focused on the topics which need to be discussed.

The best way to brainstorm is to:

- Explain the situation or problem.

- Make the goals known to all participants.

- Make notes about all elements and ideas that are discussed. Keep the notes brief.

- The list can be reviewed and refined during the brainstorming session.

- The final step would be to set a plan of action in motion.

Try to keep the sessions short, maybe 15-30 minutes total. If the session is going really well, you may let it go a little longer.

Surveys and Questionnaires

Surveys and questionnaires are another way to gather information. It is an obvious way to find out what people think about any topic. A well crafted survey or questionnaire can reveal useful information that you can use. Be sure that you do not talk over the heads of people. Make it easy to understand and clear. The questionnaires can be gathered through phone, e-mail, fax, or any other method of communication. You can also ask questions during the meeting and have someone record pertinent comments.

When you ask questions, make the problem clear and tell participants what you need to accomplish. Present the questions to attendees and keep the questionnaire less than 25 questions. The answers are more useful when you ask for demographic information about the participants. It can be good to ask the questions in several different ways, but only ask about one topic in each question. When you have the completed surveys, compile the results to see what you have learned.

We have all received phone calls with those "quick surveys" where the person asks a series of boring and usually irritating questions. It is best to avoid these type of surveys. Also try to keep the survey less than 30 minutes for the best results.

Interviews

Interviews can be a great way to gather information. You need at least two people to do an interview, one person to ask questions and another to answer them. I have done a number of interviews where a person e-mails me a questionnaire and I answer their questions. This system works but actually talking to the person will generate more in-depth answers and allows the questioner to ask follow-up questions.

There are some key times when you would want to conduct an interview. Some of these would include:

- When speaking with job applicants.

- When research is being done.

- When people are coming into the company to do training.

- When information is needed from experts in the field.

- When information needs to be collected from key people.

When you interview someone, it is important to explain why you need to speak with them. Outline the problem or area that you need information about. What do you hope to accomplish with the interview?

The questions should be prepared ahead of time and in such a way that they generate the information that is needed. Set a specific time to meet with the person or people.

When you speak to the person, they need to know some specific information.

- Who you are and why you need to speak with them.

- Tell them the reason for the interview – the goal and purpose.

- Tell the person why the information is important and why you feel they can help.

- If the meeting is confidential, let the person now.

- Explain why you chose them and what they can contribute.

- Be clear about how the information will be used and about any follow-ups.

Try to keep the interview under 30 minutes for one person. If the interviews are done with a group, you will need more time. However, limit the number of people. It is usually best to meet with only five people at one time. Before you schedule a group interview, remember that group dynamics could skew your results. Some people may say more than you need while others do not say anything with other people around. Evaluate the information you need and the people who will be interviewed. Which approach is better for the particular situation you are dealing with at the moment?

Organize

After you collect data, you need to organize it in some manner. Otherwise, the information is useless. We will discuss some of the organizing options below. Which one is right for your project?

T-Charts

A T-chart is the familiar "pro and con" list that can be used to compare information. Some of these things may include:

- Pro vs. Con

- Start vs. Stop

- Assets vs. Liabilities

- Behavior or Action compared to Benefits

- Old vs. New

These are only some of the possibilities. A T-chart can also have three columns. Three-column charts are called Double T-Charts. Use either of these to evaluate the information you collected.

Some of the benefits to these charts, include:

- Compare items or show the differences in certain information

- Show opposite thoughts or opposing possibilities

When you create a T-Chart, define the problem to be addressed and the goals you hope to reach. Draw a T-shaped frame and insert a header over the chart and headers for each column to keep the information organized. Insert each piece of information in the appropriate column. Continue until all items are entered in one column. The meeting attendees can then review the chart and analyze the information to form a plan of action.

The amount of time needed to create and review your chart will vary but watch the attendees to gauge if the meeting is going too long. Do not bore the participants. When they get tired, it is time for a break or recess until another day. You may want to meet to organize the information and allow people to take charts with them to review. At a later time you can meet again to form a plan of action.

Matrix Charts

Matrix Charts are a common way to organize information and I have used many in this book. The definition of a matrix chart states – "The Matrx Chart organizes and displays information in interrelational columns and rows." So, what does that mean?

Matrix Charts helps the group find a plan of action, make choices about the direction to be taken, keep different issues separated, evaluate the information, and chart these details in a way that others can review and understand the information.

The first priority is to determine the information you need to glean from the chart. Once you know this, plan the headings to be used across the top and left side of your chart. Fill in each spot in the center of the chart with information that applies to each heading. The information can then be used to develop a plan of action. It can take a couple of hours to develop a well thought out chart and to fill in the various elements. This is a good way to sort through duties and the people who are available to perform them. See the example below.

	Meeting Preparation	Meeting Agenda	Meeting Room Setup & Food	Meeting Room Cleanup
Bob	X			X
George		X	X	
Helen		X		X
Kate	X		X	

There are certain people who can assist with the meeting and there are specific duties that need to be handled. This chart shows who is available and what needs to be done. It is simple to put together and can easily be expanded if needed. There are many uses for this sort of chart in addition to the one shown above.

Worksheets

There are many types of worksheets that can be used to compile and organize information. The participants need to compile a worksheet to enable them to evaluate the given information and then to make a decision or form a plan of action. Usually, this sort of worksheet will only take 15 to 20 minutes to insert the relevant information. If the worksheet needs to be created and the information also needs to be inserted, it can take two or three hours for a more complicated worksheet.

Resources			
Resource	Is it Necessary?	Is it Available?	Is it Obtainable?
Energy Equipment Facility Information Interest Money People Skills Time			

This chart gives you an easy way to sort through the elements of your project to see what is available. It will also show areas where you need to gather additional information to make an informed decision.

Whatever approach you use to organize your information, remember these are basic guidelines which can be adjusted to fit your needs.

Break it Down

One of the most common ways to breakdown information is with a tree diagram. This allows you to start with one common element and then illustrate how each piece of information relates to that common element. Tree diagrams show all tasks that need to be performed and how they are interrelated and which people or departments they affect.

When your group meets to compile the chart, these are some strategic questions which need to be asked and answered.

- What needs to happen?

- What situations do we need to address?

- What do we need to resolve?

- What must be achieved to reach the goal?

A simplified way to find all elements and to arrange them in a pyramid is to write each step or element on three by five inch index cards. These cards can then be arranged and moved around until the best approach is found. When the group is happy with the plan, it can be laid out on paper.

Map It

Flow charts can be a good way to map your information. They provide a visual aid to show each step involved in a process and alternative steps in some processes. You can also use a flow chart to show how certain situations were handled successfully in the past to gather ideas on how to deal with current situations. Flow charts are a great way to illustrate the individual steps needed to accomplish goals or to solve problems. This is another project where you can list all steps on three by five inch index cards. Lay the cards out in possible processes to determine how to reach your goals. You might need to rearrange the cards in different ways to find the best system for your group.

Display It

There are times when you need to display the information that you gathered. Area graphs are one type of display. These show various values over a period of time. They show these values on a graph which shows the variations clearly. Bar graphs are another option to show values for a specific time period, or they can compare values for a time of period and compare these amounts for various periods. These can be three dimensional and use different colors to show the different values. Line graphs also show sales or other values for time periods. I have used line graphs for years to compare sales amounts for the year to date and to compare sales for different years.

SELECTED TOOLS

There are many types of tools you can use in your meetings: butcher paper, chalkboard, computer interface, flip chart, and an overhead projector. Each meeting situation calls for a different tool. This information should help you determine which tools are right for your particular situation.

Butcher Paper

Butcher paper comes in a large roll in white or brown. It is a great place to make notes and it can easily be taped to a wall.

It is best to form groups of fewer than 25 people in an informal setting. Use it to organize or display information for your group. It works well when you are brainstorming and problem solving. It is ideal for timelines or other things which require a lot of room to make notes.

This paper is easy to use and gives you a large area for notes and additions. A long piece of paper gives all attendees a chance to participate and share their thoughts. One thing I have done is include a number of people in adding notes on the paper and give each a different color marker to identify who made individual notes.

Chalkboard or Whiteboard

The board can be placed on an easel, a stand, or mounted on the wall. It is an easy way to make notes and display specific information. Be aware that permanent markers will ruin whiteboards. Post it notes can be used to mark the board in addition to notes.

Chalkboards and whiteboards are best for groups of fewer than 25 people. It is good for an informal setting where you are training or working on problem solving. The information can be erased and changed as needed. It is good to make sure someone is keeping written notes on paper for later reference. This gives you a permanent record of the information while allowing you to make changes on the board for the group.

Whiteboards and chalkboards are available at most retail stores. Consider the size of your group to be sure this tool will work for you.

Computer Interface

You will need a computer and the appropriate programs to make this possible. It is a useful tool for groups of 20–75 people. You can organize and display information on a screen through the computer to the attendees. When a person is trained to use the program, it is easy to make changes and updates, and the information can be printed out for your attendees.

Set up is simple and fast when the speaker or leader is trained to use the computer program. There is an added expense for the equipment and programs needed but regular use justifies the cost.

Flip Chart

Flip charts are basically a large note pad of blank paper which is set on an easel or other type of stand. It allows you to flip the pages as they fill up and to go back to previous pages if needed. Broad point markers in a variety of colors are great with flip charts. You can also use post it notes on the paper for special notes or to mark assignments.

Flip charts can be used to make notes before or during the meeting. It is best for a small group so that all attendees can see the notes. Use in an informal setting for people to learn and contribute to the discussion. This is a great way to make notes for the group, display information, and organize data. Highlighters can be used on these notes for extra emphasis.

Flip charts are easy to use, easy to transport, and available at any office supply store. If the speaker or meeting leader makes notes, their back will be turned to the audience while they make notes; therefore, it is best to ask someone with good handwriting to make useful notes.

Some Tips for Using Flip Charts

- **Color** – Notes are more effective when they are in different colors. Do not get crazy with the colors, but some variety or color coordinating specific topics is helpful. Black, blue, green, and purple are good for text; red, orange, and yellow are good for highlighting special notes.

- **Sticky Notes** – Stick notes on the flip chart to mark special items and details.

- **Make It Stand Out** – Some variety in the letters and numbers being used can add some interest to the notes. Use some uppercase and some lowercase. Uppercase is better for headings, title, and words that need to stand out. If your note taker is artistic, they can make shaded or hollow letters for some variety. These are just some of the ways to diversify your notes.

- **Numbers** – Lists should have numbers or some sort of bullet points to set off each item in the list.

- **Charades** – Word pictures could be useful in notes depending on the artistic ability in the group, but keep in mind the pictures need to be drawn quickly.

- **Open Space** – Do not overcrowd the pages. It is good to leave plenty of white space on your flip chart pages. Feel free to use multiple pages for a meeting.

- **Make it Stand Out** – When there are notes that you need to emphasize, underlining and circling them can be a good way to make them stand out.

Overhead Projector

Clear sheets (usually acetate) are used with overhead projectors. They can be a good way to present information to a group without the computer requirements needed for a PowerPoint presentation. You can easily make notes on the sheets with a felt tip marker.

This tool is useful for groups of 20-75 people but depends on the layout of the room. It is a good way to organize and display information to the group. The overhead projector allows you to do something similar to a flip chart but it can be visible to a larger audience.

Overhead projectors are simple to use, and most facilities or businesses have a projector available for your use. This method allows the leader to face attendees. You can use color or black and white graphics, charts, and pictures. The leader needs to be careful not to block the attendees' view. Projectors have a noisy fan, and their light bulbs need to be replaced often. Consider the lighting in the room to be sure attendees can see the information and take notes.

Graphics In Your Meeting

Graphics are a visual way to present information in your meeting. This is a great and alternative way to

- Communicate ideas
- Organize and Summarize Thoughts
- Promote Clarity in the Group
- Help Attendees have a Better Understanding

Whatever you use, it should reinforce the ideas you want to convey.

What are the main reasons you would use graphics with your group?

- Help attendees "see" the thing you are speaking about.
- Add visual and audio stimulation for the attendees.
- Simplify points for attendees that sound confusing.
- Illustrate the patterns in your ideas and processes.
- Help people have a better understanding and remember.
- The pictures can help attendees envision more than just one possibility.

Props

There are a number of props you can use in your meetings including visual aids, name tags, and basic supplies. Below are some props that can be used to add some flavor, humor, energy, drama, and aesthetics to your meeting, spurring some more creative, entertaining ideas. If you know your attendees, you should be able to gauge whether these ideas will be well received.

- **Caps or Hats** – Attendees who have specific roles or duties can wear caps or hats. This head wear can have company logo or for fun you can get decorative caps or costume hats.

- **Posters or Signs** – You can buy or create posters and signs with familiar quotes or motivational phrases and put them on the walls. You may honor attendees who contribute new, useful phrases or quotes for the meeting room in some way.

- **Gifts** – New members or guests can be given a small free gift for visiting your group, such as pens, party favors, group photos, or coffee mugs, to help them remember your group.

- **A Smiley Face** – When we were kids, many of us enjoyed being given a star for doing our chores or getting a good report card. You can do something similar with your attendees, using stickers or play money to acknowledge their contributions to the meeting. They can collect stickers to earn a gift certificate or other small gift.

- **Music** – Some meeting leaders play wordless music during their breaks or at times when the members are brainstorming or discussing items. This is effective if you play music that is agreeable to everyone.

- **Plants** – If your meeting room is good for plants, it might be nice to have live plants. They can be soothing and aesthetically pleasing. Balloons can be used for a more festive atmosphere.

13

POTENTIAL MEETING PROBLEMS

———

Effective leaders want their meetings to be productive, creative, and efficient. They should produce high levels of participation and should get commitment from your attendees. We have already discussed that this sort of meeting does not just happen. You need to make it happen. In turn, all meetings have the potential for problems. Even the best prepared and best run meeting can have problems. So, any realistic person preparing for a meeting should learn to recognize and resolve problems as they arise. Over time, meeting leaders and facilitators become better about handling difficulties.

PROBLEM SITUATIONS

There will be problems from time to time—but it is important to remember that they are people problems. These problems can include attendees who will not talk or will not stop talking, people who really do not have anything to contribute but spend a hour telling you about it, people who want to disrupt or upset the meeting, and others who want to be the center of attention.

What factors drive "people problems?" Egos, likes, dislikes, insecurities, ambitions, moods, and a wide variety of personalities. Bigger problems happen when others in the group react to the people causing the initial problems. This is a reason the leader needs to take control of problems. The leader should focus on the problems but not the people and personalities involved to keep the situation from escalating to a personal issue.

Some of the common problems you will face are mentioned below.

- **Arguments** – There are attendees who want to start a fight. It does not matter who they fight with as long as they can argue. Usually these arguments have nothing to do with your meeting. They are a convenient opportunity to start an argument.

- **Bosses** – Do you have people in your meeting who feel they are in charge? Instant disruption. Remind your attendees that each person was invited because he or she is an expert in some facet of the job, and the group needs their input. Add that one person is in charge of the meeting which will be handled in an orderly manner.

- **Incessant Talkers** – Some people will talk throughout the meeting. They whisper to the people beside them and across the table. This is disruptive to the people speaking and anyone near the talkers. One way to stop this is for the leader, facilitator, or speaker to stop talking for a few minutes to allow the attendees to finish their conversation. Glance in their direction and if they persist, some people will ask if they are finished so the meeting can proceed. That situation should be handled tactfully and will only work with some people.

- **Tardy Individuals** – Most meeting attendees have known people who are always late. I knew one habitually tardy woman who often left early but wanted to be heard while she was there. Many times she disrupted the meeting but never contributed anything. A quick way to handle this is to ask the person to have a seat quietly and mention that you will catch them up during the break. The meeting leader should deal with repeat latecomers because their behavior is rude and disruptive.

- **Meeting Black Hole** – Your attendees are bored, yawning, restless, and unproductive. What should you do to fix this problem. Have you talked about a subject too long? If so, move on and come back to it later if needed. You can find ways to clarify your point. Remind the group of the main topic and the goal you need to accomplish. Sometimes your attendees just need to be re-focused on the reason you are there.

- **Stubborn People** – We all know how irritating a person can be who gets an idea and will not let go, even when they are proven wrong. They slow down the meeting and confuse attendees because multiple topics are being discussed.

- **They Just Will not Stop** – These people usually mean well and want to contribute, but they go on and on. It can be good to work with these people to help them form their ideas and to learn to present them in concisely. The leader or facilitator can thank them for their ideas and ask if anyone else has any comments about their suggestions.

- **Unreasonable People** – Sometimes attendees have a "correct" opinion about everything .They refuse to stop talking when the leader or facilitator try to get their attention.

- **You Can Hear a Pin Drop** – What should you do when the attendees are silent? Nothing makes the meeting leaders' blood run colder than total silence. Each attendee stares at you, but no one is speaking or answering your questions. Ask yourself these questions.

  o Do the attendees need more information?

  o Should you ask the answers in a different way?

  o Did you cause the silence?

  o If so, how can you get them involved?

Games to Help You Solve Problems

Sometimes a game can be just what you need to solve problems with attendees or the meeting in general. Following are some games that could be just what you need.

Lose Barriers to Change

Why Play – Shows why people need to identify things that limit their success.

What You Need – Paper and pens

How to Play – Some of the things that can limit our effectiveness include:

- Ignoring difficult situations and decisions
- Assuming you already have all the knowledge you need on given subjects
- Generalizing your reactions
- Being overly committed to past decisions and actions
- Not considering alternatives
- Not handling stress

The items and actions listed above will limit attendees' effectiveness. After you address these details, have the group discuss these questions.

- Can you share examples of situations that fit the details listed above?
- How can people get past these problems?
- Are there specific habits that you would like to stop?
- What habits would you like to develop?
- What restrains you in your work environment?
- What would help you evaluate these restraints?

Make four lists on your paper. Label them: rigid, flexible, real, and imaginary. Under each of these labels, list the constraints in your life under the correct label. Carefully evaluate each constraint in view of which category they fall into.

Myths

Why Play – This shows how easy it is to believe myths.

What You Need –Nothing

How to Play – Explain the term myth—"A fiction or half truth that appeals to the consciousness of people while expressing deep, commonly felt emotions."

Give attendees some common myths to consider. These can include

- Everybody does it.
- One size fits all.
- Age is all in your mind.
- The government is here to help you.
- The check is in the mail.

There are many more and you can feel free to add your own. Other common myths can be the belief that the product or service you are offering will sell itself. Let attendees think about this and ask these questions.

- What helps to perpetuate these beliefs?
- Where did the myth originate?
- How can we end the myth?
- Is it a myth or is it true?

Change is Part of Life

Why Play – Help the group learn that change is necessary and how it is easier to work with changes rather than fight them.

What You Need – Pens, paper, pencils

How to Play – Divide into groups of four or five people. It works better if the people are from different areas of the business. The groups need to discuss the following questions:

- What was a recent change in your workplace?
- Did people resist the change?
- Why? Why not?
- How could people have made the change easier?

Give them time to discuss the questions.

CONFLICTS

Some conflict in meetings will drive the discussion and generate useful information. These conflicts can be caused by competitive feelings, differences between people, or rivalry.

If the conflict is contained and managed, it can bring positive results.

- Greater motivation among the attendees.
- More creative thinking which generates diversified points of view.
- Better understanding of the agenda topics.
- Forcing people to explain their point of view.

This section is about what happens when conflicts get out of control and problems are allowed to escalate.

The Cause

One common conflict will surface when different groups of people come to your meeting with preconceived ideas. It becomes more intense when they are unwilling to be open minded and evaluate the situation from other point of views. These are the most common situations which cause conflict to escalate.

- **Miscommunication** – Many people do not listen to each other, failing to understand what is being said.

- **Observation** – Two different people can see the same thing in different ways. This can be even worse when there are multiple people in the group who see the situation differently.

- **Preferred Developments** – Different people can want various things to happen when a situation is resolved or a problem is solved.

- **Values** – People decide what they feel is acceptable or proper based on their personal values which may vary greatly.

Understand the Conflict

If the meeting leader understands the conflict, it is easier to manage. The way you deal with conflict has a major impact on the attendees and the overall success of your meeting. It can also affect how participants deal with each other in future meetings. There are five basic ways to approach this problem. The situation will dictate which approach should be used in each situation. Keep in mind that at times, you have to use the complicated solution, rather than the easy and comfortable way. The easy way out can lead to many other more complicated problems over time.

- **Avoidance** – Some conflicts do not need to be resolved right away. When it is trivial, there is no reason to make the situation worse. It is wise to watch the situation and see if more involvement is needed.

- **Strike a Bargain** – This is a good way to compromise when an ideal solution is not possible. It works well when each side is willing to give a little. Let them decide what they are willing to give up and what they feel is non negotiable and start there. Usually, each party can make some concessions while retaining particular concerns.

- **Make Demands** – People who approach conflict by demanding their way are self-centered, There will be a winner and a loser. Meeting leaders need to head off situations that will divide the group.

- **Give In** – This is the option that will help preserve the group relationship, and the person giving in shows that the well being of the group is important to them. You can help participants find a way to give in or make a sacrifice while still saving face with their peers.

- **Solve Problems** – This approach can maintain the relationship along with winning. The people involved work together to find a solution that works for each of them. Finding the solution is only the first step. There needs to be a creative solution and follow-up. When your group has problems, which of these methods do you prefer?
  - Confronting the Conflict
  - Finding a Compromise
  - Smoothing Ruffled Feathers and Hurt Feelings
  - Showing the Attendees Who's in Charge
  - Forming a Coalition to Find a Solution

DEAL WITH PROBLEMATIC PARTICIPANTS

There are times when you need to deal with problematic and difficult meeting participants. Keeping your meeting moving and active can eliminate many potential problems, but some participants may feel the need to monopolize the meeting, distract others, and refuse to participate in the meeting. Here are some ways to work with them to get their behavior under control.

- **Encourage New People** – Some attendees may hesitate to participate when the group could benefit from their comments.

Try posing a question and asking how many people have comments about that topic. When new hands are raised, you can call on individuals to share their thoughts. You may find that it is good to "plant" questions with quiet or hesitant attendees before the meeting. This gives them time to prepare an answer and get ready to participate without being put on the spot.

- **Is It That Bad** – Some individual know how to "push our buttons." We need to be careful about overreacting to moderately bad behavior. Does the behavior really qualify as troublesome? If the person is a nuisance, it can be good meet privately after the meeting. Some people will stop being a problem when they realize that you are going to keep the meeting going and refuse to let them disrupt it.

- **It Is That Bad** – When behavior really is bad, it is up to the leader to deal with it – in private. If the behavior has gotten out of control, you might need to stop the meeting for a few minutes and make it clear to the group that this is not acceptable. Stand firm and retake control of the meeting and the group.

- **It Is Not Personally** – Remember that in most instances bad behavior is not directed at you personally. If you find it is personal, it needs to be handled in private and should involve a supervisor to support your actions.

- **Listen to Attendees** – Meeting leaders need to listen, even when the person is on a tangent. It is useful to interrupt them and summarize important parts. Specifically ask another person to speak or respond after thanking the person for their input.

- **Make Changes** – If problems persist, change the way participation is handled. Break the group into pairs or smaller groups instead of a large group. The smaller groups also give the troublemakers a smaller audience so they can be reined in.

- **Nonverbal** – Many times the leader can make eye contact with the person causing a problem. It might be good to move closer to people who are talking to others during the meeting or who start to doze off. It is good to establish hand signals to let participants know they need to wrap up a comment.

- **Personal Touch** – Take the time to get to know attendees who cause problems before the meeting, after the meeting, or during breaks. This is a good technique when attendees cause problems or are withdrawn. Show an interest in them and try to find a way to make them a contributing part of the group.

- **Rules** – It may be necessary to create rules about group participation. These can include the following ideas or variations of these. People may have only one chance to contribute their thoughts on a topic. You can instruct attendees that their comments need to build on previous comments. Each attendee should give their personal thoughts without trying to speak for others.

GET BACK ON TRACK

These are some common ways to settle conflicts and get the meeting back on track.

- Make the objectives clear to all attendees.

- Keep the group focused on the facts and any information that supports them.

- It could be best to stop the discussion for the time being.

- Sometimes some tactful and well placed humor will do the trick, but be sure the person can handle humor. Otherwise the situation could get worse.

- Find alternatives. Are there other ways to reach a decision? This would be a good time for "Plan B."

- It is good to be understanding. Take the time to listen and work to understand what the other person is saying to you.

When the group is stuck on a problem or you get the feeling you have hit a brick wall, switch gears briefly and give everyone a chance to regroup. Many times that is all it takes to loosen everyone up and to get ideas flowing again. When I was conducting business meetings on a regular basis, I kept a notebook that I took to every meeting. I had 10 pages of sayings to use at the end of the meetings and a list ideas to get the group to get creative. It is amazing how a little change can help your attendees think of new ways to approach a situation. Which of these ideas will work for your group?

- **Take a Slow, Deep Breath** – Ask all attendees to take 10 slow, deep breaths. They should inhale deeply and exhale deeply. These are cleansing breaths which can help refresh the body and mind.

- **Say it Again** – Have attendees call out names of books or movies. To give them more of a challenge, ask for a specific actor actress, director, studio, or writer. Give them one minute to call out as many as possible.

- **Take a Break** – Sometimes you just need to give your attendees a short break. Let them get a drink, stretch their legs, and get out of the meeting room for a few minutes. If you are in a place where they can walk outside and breathe fresh air—even better.

- **Musical Chairs** – If the meeting goes stagnant, have attendees switch seats. This idea works even better when they move to a different part of the room. They can move from one side to the other and get a different perspective on the room and on the topics you are talking about.

- **Make Notes** – Sometimes you need to stop the conversation and have attendees write down a few ideas. Having them use their non dominant hand can open the mind. If you have artistic people in your group, let them draw an idea instead of putting it into words.

- **Change the Lighting** – Turn the lights off, dim the lights or make them brighter. A change in the lighting can make people see things differently and open their mind. The same is true with the temperature in the room. Do not make it too hot or too cold, but a moderate change can make a difference.

- **Change the Topic** – When the group is really stuck, sideline a specific topic and move on to something different. You can always come back to a difficult topic at another time if necessary.

FIND SOLUTIONS

When the problems are discovered, it is critical to find solutions. Any issues need to be handled quickly and effectively. The longer problems drag on the more people feel it is acceptable to cause problems and the more they disrupt the meetings.

Games to Find Solutions to Problems

Here are a couple of games that your group can play to find solutions to problems within the group or with attendees.

Share The Wealth

Why Play – Help attendees share ideas with each other.

What You Need – Five three by five inch index cards for each attendee

How to Play – Before the meeting begins, propose a problem for the group. Have attendees submit five good solutions to one person before the meeting. These need to be written on three by five inch index cards. Attendees need to write their name on the back of these cards. A master list needs to be made with all the suggestions. Pass out copies of the master list at the meeting and have each attendee mark their 10 favorite ideas. The votes should be tabulated and a small prize will be given to the person who submitted the winning idea. This will get their creative juices flowing and also gave them all sorts of additional possibilities to the problem.

Stop Wasting Time

Why play – To help attendees identify the biggest time wasters in their day and find ways to limit how much time they waste.

What You Need – Transparency, overhead projector handout, paper, pens, and pencils

How to Play – Ask e attendees to think about how time seems to fly and how that affects how much they get done. Have them list the top ten time wasters they can think of. Divide participants into groups of three and have them compare lists. Which time wasters did they have in common? List these on a transparency and share with the group. What are the biggest time wasters in your area? What suggestions do they have to limit the amount of time that is wasted? How does your list compare to the list below?

Common Time Wasters:

- Personal or business crises
- Doing too many things at once
- Telephone calls
- Ineffective delegation
- Visitors dropping in
- No self-discipline
- Procrastination
- Not being able to say "No"
- Disorganization

CASE STUDY

From a leader's perspective, recognize and identify problem areas in meeting content that affect the overall health of the organization. It is advantageous to identify them and work toward resolution. Working in group settings such as a city council, allows for diversity in opinion to promote healthy conversations. Problematic issues or conflicts in meetings should be recognized as "opportunities" to create a more comprehensive base of conversation that will inevitably lead to more effective policy-making.

It is critical that the leader can manage a meeting efficiently, focus on topics and present issues objectively. As conflicts arise, the leader should be well versed in organizational structure to ensure that matters are properly referred to the appropriate personnel for resolution. Whether the issue is resolved, it is important to value those who bring issues forward. You will find that people appreciate being heard and respected.

Interpersonal relation skills are critical in setting the tone for any organization.

Meetings can be plagued with disruption, depending upon the volatility of the issues at hand. Leadership is again key in managing these situations. The leader of any group should manage according to *Roberts Rules of Order*. This will ensure that consistency prevails in managing those in the group as well as the audience so that you can defend requiring people to observe protocol and comment appropriately through set procedures. If a meeting has an adverse issue on the agenda, it is best for the chairperson to set the parameters for commenting in terms of time allowed and speaking more than once. It is always helpful to have a sign-up sheet available before the meeting for potential speakers. Efficiency in dealing with conflicts or disruptions should always be process oriented.

Keeping your meeting productive is critical. Rely on your agenda when moving from one issue to the next. Your chairperson should allow discussion among board or committee members. In elected groups, this is their opportunity to represent their constituency and weigh in with their own opinions. Again, your leadership is key in moving the agenda along ensuring that every item has been discussed at an appropriate level.

Healthy organizations will have a "reflective" or "feedback" session with their managers or group members. Primarily, this allows you to reflect on the meeting, identify problems that require solutions, and set your future direction. These sessions are valuable for creating a strong base to work from within your organization. They also give an opportunity for other people to weigh in on the issues at hand and take responsibility for resolution. Organizationally, this promotes teamwork and keep everyone focused on priorities.

Lorie Smith
Former School Board Leader
Waynesboro, VA City Councilwoman

14

HOW TO END
A MEETING

In Chapter 7 we talked about the importance of starting your meeting correctly, but ending your meeting properly is just as important. Some meetings end and no one is quite sure if they are over. I've been to some meetings that ended when the leader stopped talking, but there was no wrap up, no summary, and the attendees did not adjourn. It just stopped. A meeting needs a conclusion.

I have chosen to offer a quote for the day. My attendees knew the quote was a way to end the meeting and to send them on their way with something positive to consider. I collected a adages and tried to find one appropriate for the information in the meeting.

ACHIEVE A CONSENSUS

Earlier in the book we discussed ways to generate ideas and find possible solutions to problems. However, is it enough to generate a list of possibilities? A thorough meeting produces possible ideas, but the participants should also reach a consensus on which idea to implement. An action plan to implement ideas is a great way to wrap up your meeting.

If there is no need to make changes, why was the meeting called in the first place? In some cases, the decision must be made by someone higher in the company, but the group can elaborate on the ideas developed in the meeting to help supervisors when they make a final decision.

Imagine a meeting with intense brainstorming but the meeting suddenly ended? What a letdown for the participants who worked hard to create suggestions!

Problem solving meetings should have a resolution. Not all meetings require final decisions and a consensus such as those below.

- Social Meetings

- Team Building Meetings

- Training Meetings

Autocratic Decisions

There are some situations where one person makes the final decision and he or she has already done so. Why call a meeting and ask for suggestions? Leaders who call a meeting and ask for ideas should make their intentions clear. If you ask for ideas, tell the participants how their feedback will be used, processed, who will review it, and when you expect to make a decision. This sort of information can make people more willing to put time and effort into offering suggestions. Remember that most ideas and suggestions require effort from others not in attendance.

If a boss routinely calls meetings to ask for ideas and never uses any of the suggestions, it can hurt morale in the group. It is much better to acknowledge their contribution and there can be valuable suggestions which may come from unexpected sources.

Have you been in a meeting where a problem is posed and almost immediately a boss makes a solution? Attendees agree that it has definite potential and is approved right away. The problem is that some attendees may have concerns but decide to stay quiet. They may feel its better not to "rock the boat." The result is that the problem is not evaluated thoroughly.

Working Together to Reach a Consensus

To reach an educated consensus, the group needs to ask questions and discuss the idea in detail. It takes longer in the early stages but will save unnecessary reworking later. The group will discover more options, analyze alternatives which are more plausible, and then find the best possible solution. When the group works together to find the best answer, the group wins and the individuals feel good about their contribution. Everyone will feel that contributed and all angles were evaluated before the final decision was reached.

How does your group reach a consensus? This might be one of the most mysterious facets of meeting procedures. A consensus can only be reached through discussion. It is built in pieces as each idea is generated and evaluated by the group. These are some of the characteristics of a group that will reach a consensus.

- All participants are involved. They understand that they can expect to contribute useful information to the process. Some ideas will be more raw than others, but the group will work together and add details to the ideas being considered.

- The points that your group agrees on need to be summarized by the leader or facilitator. Ideas that everyone agrees on should be noted along with areas of concern. Any concerns can be discussed further.

- The group should discuss positive and negative aspects of any idea. All group members should be encouraged to state their concerns.

- When the group has an idea for a solution that contains potential problems, they need to be discussed in more detail.

It will be obvious when the group has a consensus. The concerns will be worked out and the solution along with a plan of action will take shape, and the group will agree on it. The facilitator or leader needs to recognize when the group reaches this point. When the group is near the point of reaching a consensus, the following questions can be asked to confirm where the group is in the process.

- "Where do we stand on the decision about ____? Does anyone have additional concerns that we need to discuss?"

- "Is everyone in agreement? If not, what additional information do we need to cover?"

- "We can move to the next part of the agenda, unless anyone has other questions."

- "Is there anything in this solution that we do not feel confident presenting to the supervisors?"

A consensus should not be a compromise. When people compromise they give up key elements that are important to them. When a true consensus is reached, each person in the group feels comfortable with the final decisions. No one should give up points they feel are important. For this to happen, each person in the group must speak honestly and freely with the other participants.

Some Methods to Reach a Consensus

Here are some techniques you can use to reach a consensus in your meetings.

If you begin with 10 to 15 choices, narrow it down to five for manageability. This is the process to use.

- List all options on a flip chart. Combine similar options to create less choices.

- Let the participants take a few minutes to consider the list.

- Let each participant cast a ballot for each option that sounds possible to them. They can vote for more than one, but should not vote for all choices.

- Tally the ballots and discuss the remaining choices. At that point vote again and eliminate more choices. Keep narrowing the list down until you make a final choice.

- If time is limited, let each attendee vote for one or two methods they like best. The vote can be on paper or by a show of hands. Repeat until you narrow the list down to a manageable size. Once the list is shortened, the group should discuss the remaining choices in more detail.

Start Small

It is easier to reach a conclusion with a small group. That is the principle that makes this method effective.

- Review the issue that is under discussion and address some of the ideas and thoughts that have been shared by the group.

- Ask participants for their thoughts about the review.

- Separate the group members into smaller groups.

- Each group needs to pick one person to present their proposal to the group.

- Each proposal should be listed on a flip chart or other board.

- The larger group can then discuss the ideas submitted by the small groups.

- The smaller groups go back to work on areas where there is a debate.

- Once the debate is handled, the smaller group presents their proposal again.

Polling the Group

Polling is a good way to gauge the group and see how far apart the attendees are in making a decision. This will also indicate what points need to be discussed in more detail before there can be a resolution.

- Notify all participants that no more ideas will be presented or accepted on a particular topic.

- Review the plan and explain the steps to reach a consensus. The participants may accept the plan, decide the plan is fair, disagree with the plan, disagree with the decision, or may express their concerns about the proposed plan.

- Make a list of the possible ideas on the flip chart. Each attendee needs to state their thoughts on these ideas. A simple head count can work.

- When the results are tallied, announce them to the group. This will show you what ideas need to be discussed in more detail.

- Ask the attendees for their comments. Even if only one person has an issue with the idea, listen to that person.

Will any of these techniques help your group reach a consensus? Are there ways to make adjustments to these ideas to make them work for your group? I like to take a variety of ideas and create methods that work for a specific group of people. You never know what idea will spark the best possibilities for your meeting.

Maintain Individuality within the Group

When a group of people works together for a long time, they begin to have groupthink. This has its good and bad points. They will work in sync which is beneficial, but members may stop expressing their personal thoughts about projects and just go along with the group which cuts its effectiveness.

Another situation where this can happen is when the people making the decisions are too far removed from the day-to-day operations of the business. This happens when a board of directors makes decisions without sufficient input from people who work on the projects. Here are the reasons we talked about the importance of inviting the right people to your meetings. Which people have personal knowledge of details that need to be considered? These people need to be at the meeting and should have the freedom to contribute these details.

One other time when members suppress their thoughts is when the group wants to wrap the meeting up even though the problems may not be resolved, and the decisions may not be made. The meeting could be running late or there is pressure to make a decision. When there is a lot of pressure for a decision, people may keep concerns to themselves to get a quicker resolution without taking the time to get the best solution.

These tips can help your group keep from falling into this trap.

- Create a diverse group with various experience and backgrounds.

- Group members need to have different points of view.

- The leader or facilitator needs to make attendees feel comfortable enough to share their thoughts about topics being discussed in your meeting.

- Decisions should be postponed until the group feels good about the resolution.

- Get the opinions of other people who have useful information to share.

- Listen to the input being offered in a positive manner.

BEFORE THE MEETING ENDS

One huge attendee complaint is that meetings do not end on time. Doing so helps the group maintain their commitment, enthusiasm, and positive attitude about your group and their goals. When leaders let meetings run over their time limit, they indicate that they do not value their attendees' time.

People have mentioned that long meetings are a reason they do not volunteer for groups. In a business situation, employees may have no choice about attending meetings. Never-ending meetings seldom accomplish their group's goals. There are two options—end the meeting on time or discuss how much additional time is needed and find a solution with the participants. Your group need to determine the following information before the end of your meeting.

- **What Needs to be Done** – Be specific about what to do. The more specific instructions are, the less possibility of confusion. Some of these things could include additional research and information, finding or requesting additional funding, writing a proposal, hiring or bringing in additional people, or actually starting the project.

- **When Does it Need to be Done** – It is good to set a realistic timetable. Within the time table, there should be checkpoints or goals to be reached to keep the team motivated and indicate progress is being made. Include information about how the timeline will be handled and monitored.

- **Who Will Be Responsible** – Assign each part of the action plan to someone before adjourning the meeting. Attendees can be volunteers or the meeting leader can handpick people if needed. Assignees need to agree to the terms for the project.

Have you ever been in a meeting and you had a great idea, but you were afraid to bring it up because you knew the task would be assigned to you? This is not rare. I've even started some comments with, "This is an idea that might work, but I am currently tied up with other projects." In a group, you should have some "idea" people, while other people can form and implement a plan of action. A leader or facilitator can motivate their people by not trying to force an assignment on the wrong person. Give people the opportunity to volunteer first and then assign projects if there are not enough volunteers.

END THE MEETING

How many times were you in a meeting that ended on time? It can be a rare event and many attendees are shocked when it happens. One way to end on time is to stop on time no matter what is happening, but that y is not the most effective way to end on time.

A better way to end the meeting on time is to monitor each segment of the meeting. I list times beside each agenda item. Schedules can include starting or ending time to keep you on track. If one segment runs over, another needs to be cut. Be careful that some parts of the meeting are not cut too short. Your timing will improve when a conscious effort is made to start and end on time. Even if the meeting starts late, it should still end on time.

Ending meetings on time shows that the leader and facilitator are organized, prepared, and have respect for attendees.

CASE STUDY

It is always "best practice" to lead a group to consensus on all matters. Achieving consensus is not always the easiest path to take, but it is one of the primary responsibilities in bringing issues to closure. Working toward consensus requires conversation that may be diverse. However, after all viewpoints are considered, most groups I find that middle ground that all can accept. Realistically, there will be issues that will be voted up or down where consensus cannot be reached. Appropriate discussion with everyone being heard signifies a healthy organization even if there are unresolved issues.

Working to end your meeting is truly a function of your agenda. Agendas should be topic oriented and your chairperson should work through it efficiently. Meetings should always be structured and provide ample time for discussion. There will inevitably be issues that need to be revisited or tabled for future meetings, another tool available to bring matters to a close.

Lorie Smith
Former School Board Leader
Waynesboro, VA City Councilwoman

15

EVALUATE AND ASSESS
A MEETING

———

Why do you want feedback? It is the best way to find out how you need to improve and what you are doing well. Meeting attendees are in the best position to give you honest, constructive criticism. However, the most important thing is a desire to make needed improvements. No matter how much feedback you receive, nothing will improve until you are motivated to make it better.

Your first priority is to determine what needs to be improved. This is why you need feedback from attendees. It can be verbal or written. Later in this chapter there are sample feedback forms that you can use or change to suit your purposes. Review the forms and see what people mention that should be improved. If a number of people mention one thing, you need to consider the suggestion. You may ask for suggestions about how to make changes. Here are the steps to making the needed improvements.

- Find the motivation to make the needed changes.

- Collect feedback about the existing meetings.

- Determine what elements of the meeting need work.

- Determine the best way to make the needed changes.

- Use the new method and evaluate whether that was the correct change.

OFFER BETTER FEEDBACK

Feedback helps anyone identify how they can make meetings more effective It is much easier to ask others whether you are making your point. This is the process that helps people hone their meeting skills to be more effective. It is critical to offer feedback in a positive way. I've found that no matter how bad something is, you can always find something positive to say.

Tips for More Effective Feedback

The way you word your comments will also make a big difference in how the comments are received.

- **Offer Examples** – Give examples of the problems.

- **Be Specific** – Make these comments specific.

- **Mention Things That Can be Changed** – Offer comments about things that can be fixed.

- **Timing is Everything** – It is good to let the person know as soon as possible. Mention the problem while it is fresh in everyone's mind.

- **Make it Clear** – Speak clearly and make the point clear. If the person does not understand, word it differently.

In most cases there are two definite ways to word things. Here are a few examples.

Bad Wording	More Effective Wording
You are unprofessional.	You could speak in a more professional manner and conduct the meeting more efficiently.
You are disgusting and obnoxious.	Some people find your stories embarrassing.
You are a snob.	I feel overlooked or unimportant. Is there a reason you invited me to the meeting?

You are rude.	The next time we discuss this problem, will you give me a chance to finish my thought?
You are self centered.	Do you understand and appreciate the information and background that I bring to the meetings? I can offer helpful insights.
You like to degrade others.	I do not feel like you really take the time to listen and consider what I have to offer.
The meeting was handled wrong.	I was discouraged that we could not reach a decision or solve the problem. We can find the answer at the next meeting.
You are great.	Thank you so much for helping me with that situation.

You are basically saying the same thing, but the effect is different. Your words, tone, and body language make a difference. The wording suggested above will help you make a positive comment that should be taken as constructive criticism meant to help.

CHECKLISTS TO COLLECT FEEDBACK

Checklists can be handed out at the end of the meeting or along with other handouts for the meeting. Attendees can return them before they leave or later. If they take them out of the meeting, you may need to follow-up with them. You can call people and get their feedback on the telephone. An e-mail or fax response would work. Do you feel it would be helpful to explain why the feedback forms are important? These are the common reasons why people want feedback from the people in attendance.

- The meeting leader has a desire to make the necessary changes.

- Attendees are given a chance to share their honest viewpoint of the meeting.

- The leader plans to use the feedback by making the needed changes.

- The attendees have the chance to share their thoughts in a positive way.

This section contains a variety of forms. You can use these forms or use pieces of the various forms to create your own. Find the elements that you think would be the most beneficial for your group. Be honest about the feedback you need and accept the answers submitted by the attendees.

This is a variation of a popular feedback form that I have filled out after many meetings. It gives you the chance to rate the meeting with a numeric score based on various elements of the meeting.

MEETING RATING CHECKLIST		
At the end of the meeting, review the following statements and put a check beside each one that you feel applies to this meeting.	YES	NO
1. I received a copy of the agenda to review before the meeting.		
2. Attendees were allowed to give feedback about the agenda and it was considered.		
3. Attendees were given the place and time for the meeting in advance.		
4. The meeting room was laid out in a good manner and the room was comfortable.		
5. The meeting started at the pre-determined time.		
6. The agenda indicated a projected time for the meeting to end.		
7. Each segment of the meeting had an established time frame.		
8. All attendees were given a chance to state their thoughts and suggestions.		
9. All attendees paid attention to the discussion and meeting topics.		
10. The leader or facilitator did periodic summaries as the meeting progressed.		
11. Everyone participated.		

12. All attendees were given a chance to participate in the discussion and decision.		
13. I feel the meeting accomplished the goals which were outlined on the agenda.		
14. Attendees were asked for their thoughts about the meeting after it concluded.		
15. I feel the attendees will follow through with the decisions made at the meeting.		
16. A memo was supplied to meeting attendees after the meeting.		
17. The leader took time to talk with participants after the meeting to follow-up.		
18. All pertinent people attended the meeting.		
19. The leader made the correct decision making procedure.		
20. All equipment was prepared and used properly at the meeting.		

Count the number of "yes" marks and multiply by 5. Check the meeting rating below.

80–100 = An effective and quality meeting which benefits the attendees

60–79 = The meeting was handled well, but improvement is needed.

0–59 = The meeting leadership needs additional training and changes are needed.

RATE EFFECTIVE OF TODAY'S MEETING		
Group:	Date:	
Rate various elements of the meeting based on a scale of 1–5. The ratings are 1 = unacceptable, 2 = below average, 3 = average, 4 = above average, and 5 = great. Circle your choice.		
1. Was the meeting effective?		1 2 3 4 5
2. Did the meeting start on time?		1 2 3 4 5
3. Did the right people attend?		1 2 3 4 5
4. Was the meeting fun?		1 2 3 4 5
5. Did the meeting meet its goals?		1 2 3 4 5
6. Were attendees prepared?		1 2 3 4 5
7. Was feedback encouraged?		1 2 3 4 5
8. Was the facilitator effective?		1 2 3 4 5
9. Was action taken?		1 2 3 4 5
10. Was the agenda was effective?		1 2 3 4 5
11. Was a consensus reached?		1 2 3 4 5
12. Were elements organized?		1 2 3 4 5
What else can be done to make future meetings more effective? Please list any additional comments.		

Ask yourself some questions about your meetings. This process only works if you are honest. It can help you pinpoint problems.

EVALUATE YOUR MEETINGS		
At the end of the meeting, review the following statements and put a check beside each one that you feel applies.	YES	NO
1. We make quality and effective decisions.		
2. We find better resolutions when the group brainstorms the problems.		
3. The attendees feel good about the decisions we make.		
4. Discussing things in a group creates a team atmosphere.		
5. All members of the group share their thoughts and opinions.		
6. Our leaders take us through the questions will skill and ease.		
7. We do not have meetings unless they are really needed.		
8. Our meetings always end on time.		
9. Our participants have a chance to share unusual ideas and suggestions.		
10. The leader keeps us focused on the agenda.		
11. Our meetings tend to make our team more united in our work.		
12. Meeting dominate most of our work days.		
13. The meetings take too much time and are not worth the time.		
14. We do not usually find the answers we need.		
15. The discussion does not reach a conclusion.		
16. The meetings just take us away from more important work.		
17. One person could find a better solution in less time.		
18. The leader discussed unrelated topics not on the agenda.		

19. We have far too many meetings.		
20. Several attendees seem to overshadow everyone else at the meeting.		

These questions help you determine –

- If the meeting was needed.

- If the meeting worked toward a reasonable conclusion.

- Whether attendees were given a chance to give their thoughts and suggestions.

- Whether attendees will feel good about the effectiveness of the meeting.

- If the meeting was efficient and effective.

- The quality of the meeting and its accomplishments.

FIND OUT HOW YOU DID

Evaluating effectiveness of your meetings is crucial to success. There are many ways you can evaluate a meeting and we will review a number of them. I cannot tell you which one is better for you. That answer depends on your group and your leadership skills. It is good to try different ideas until you find the one that works best for you.

Most feedback will come from the participants. Some of these people will give you verbal feedback as they are racing out the door. You can ask participants for their thoughts before they leave. These are some questions to ask them.

- Did you read the agenda before the meeting?

- Did you prepare any information to share at the meeting?

- Did you share useful ideas and thoughts with the group?

- Do you understand your responsibilities based on the results of the meeting?

- What can we do to make preparation easier for future meetings?

- What can and should be improved in upcoming meetings?

Verbal Feedback

An easy way to gather feedback is through hand gestures. A thumb pointed up for a good meeting. Thumb pointing to the side for a so-so meeting or a thumb pointed down for a bad meeting. At this point, you can have the participants write down their thoughts or share them with the group. Whatever you decide, it is important to hear from the people who offered a thumb turned down for a bad meeting. For more detailed and specific feedback, ask for an opinion of various portions of the meeting.

I've been to some meetings where it ends with each member sharing a couple of words about their favorite part of the meeting. You could also ask about the least favorite parts of the meeting, or simply ask for attendee comments on the meeting.

The meeting facilitator may want to ask questions to get more details from the attendees. Some of these may include the following.

- What worked well in the meeting?

- What did not work well in the meeting?

- What could be improved?

- Are there any specific suggestions for ways to make improvements?

- How could the agenda be improved?

- How could more participation be generated?

The answers may be vague, but a good leader or facilitator can ask follow-up questions to get to the more specific information that is needed to make real improvements. Someone should be chosen to take names and record comments so that interviews can follow. It is good to end the feedback session with at least one clear way to make the next meeting better.

Written Feedback

Earlier in this chapter I provided some examples of feedback forms. These are just samples and can be changed to suit your needs. These are some distinct advantages to gathering written feedback.

- People are usually more open and honest in writing than they are verbally and to your face.

- Some people express themselves better when they take a few minutes to form the words on paper.

- The written forms can be kept and there is no chance of making incorrect notes as happens during a lively conversation.

- More information can be gathered on a form

- The form can be tailored to your group to gather the information you need.

These forms are relatively simple to compile and should be easy to complete. Multiple choice is a favorite of mine because it is easy to answer. There are many types of scales that can be used. Here are a few.

- Good, fair, bad

- 1–5, 1 being bad and 5 being good

- The Likert scale can be used and it includes: strongly agree, agree, disagree, and strongly disagree. Or you can use: always, almost always, sometimes, rarely, and never. Five point scales are the most common.

When you create your custom forms, you can combine the multiple choice answers that are offered. However, this can get complicated. You might want to group all questions with the same answer options together to make it easier for the attendees to understand and complete. It can also be good to leave the room for attendees to add their own comments under the individual questions.

Keep in mind there are some disadvantages to using a written form for your feedback. These are some of those problems.

- You must decipher the writing of some attendees.
- It can be more complicated to share written thoughts with attendees.
- A person needs to take time to review the feedback forms and compile the information.

These are reasons to evaluate whether it is better to gather verbal or written feedback. Which method would be better for your group? You can use one method and then make changes if needed.

When you create questions to gather feedback, there are basic things you need to learn. The following is a selection of questions to choose the ones that will work best for your group. It is also good to change the questions from time to time instead of using the same questions at every meeting.

- Was the agenda circulated early enough for adequate preparation?
- Did everyone arrive on time?
- If not, what could be changed to help people arrive on time?
- Did attendees get sufficient notice about the meeting?
- Was the agenda organized and suitable for the meeting goals?
- Was an adequate room used for the meeting?
- If not, what changes should be made in the location?
- Did the meeting start on time?
- Was the goal of the meeting made clear from the beginning?
- Was only one topic discussed at a time?
- Did everyone in the meeting participate?

- Was their participation on topic and useful?

- Did more than one person talk at a time?

- What could be done to ensure that only one person has the floor at a time?

- Did attendees feel they could speak their mind?

- Do the attendees show respect for each other and the meeting process?

- Were questions used in the right way and to further understanding of the topic?

- If not, how could this be improved?

- Were points summarized after each section of the meeting?

- Were the discussions applicable to the topics on the agenda?

- Did the group review the positive and negative aspects of all topics?

- Were they discussed sufficiently?

- Were decisions made fairly and only after adequate discussion?

- Did the meeting progress at a reasonable pace?

- Was the entire agenda discussed or were parts skipped to end on time?

- Did the meeting reach the goals that were set out in the beginning?

- If not, what could be done to ensure this was accomplished at the next meeting?

- Were all action plans and assignments made clear for the attendees?

- Were the assignments fair and equal?

- Were plans for the next meeting mentioned?

- What was the overall atmosphere of the meeting?

- Did the meeting end on time?

These are just some of the things you might want to ask. Remember, questions should be tailored to fit the problems that pertain to your group.

Once you ask the pointed questions, you can also shift to more open-ended questions. After you have the specific information you want, you may want to ask: are there any other comments, observations, or recommendations before we end the discussion? You do need input and feedback, but do not let the discussion go on too long. In instances where you have ongoing problems, it could be best to schedule a session just to discuss problems in the meetings and how to fix them. This can save a lot of frustrations and headaches at future meetings.

MEETING MINUTES

Minutes for the meeting are an important part of follow-up. A good minute taker is critical for your meeting. There are different ways to prepare the minutes. Some simply a series of statements about what happened at the meeting. However, effective minutes can capture the essence of your meeting. They show in clear words what was accomplished by the attendees and explain the action being taken by the group. These are also easy to read and understand. The notes should be compiled in a way that is representative of the group and the way the meeting is handled.

The finished minutes need to include the following information.

1. Date, time, and location.

2. All participants by name and you may want to include their department or expertise. This is especially useful for guests and visitors.

3. Name each person who was invited but did not attend to give a more complete view of the original meeting that was planned.

4. List which participants handled particular duties. These include: leader, facilitator record keeper, scribe, and time keeper.

5. Include the complete agenda.

6. There needs to be a complete report about each portion of the agenda. Include main topics that were discussed and the outcome. Along with the outcome, include a list of the people responsible for implementing the action plan and the estimated time for completion of the plan. What results are expected?

7. List topics that will be discussed at future meeting. It could be useful to give reasons that they were not handled at this meeting, if applicable.

8. Include an honest and adequate assessment of the meeting and attach any reports or visual aids that were handed out at the meeting.

It is best to use a simple format for the minutes that can be used as a template. After each meeting, the up-to-date information can be entered into the template. Decisions and any action plan information should stand out on the minutes. The template also gives you consistency which makes it easier for attendees to find appropriate information when they review the minutes.

Experts say the minutes should be distributed the following day or two to three days later. The record keeper needs to understand that minutes are a priority. A quick turnaround will help the attendees know that the meeting and the records are a priority. Compiling the minutes should not be overly complicated making it easier for the note keeper to compose the notes for the group. These notes will be circulated to the people who missed the meeting, so be sure they have enough information for absentees to understand what happened.

The meeting leader might be involved in helping to determine which people need these minutes. Besides everyone who was in attendance and attendees who missed the meeting, anyone who supervises the attendees needs a copy of the minutes, since it involves the person's work, as well as any people who will be affected by the decisions from the meeting or who will be involved in the action plan.

Once the minutes are complete and the list of recipients is ready, the minutes need to be distributed. This can be done through e-mail, fax, interoffice mail memo, or another useful manner which is fast, easy, and free if possible. Another simple possibility is to post the minutes on a page of the company Web site. This page can have limited access so that only the people who need access can open the page.

The record keeper needs to file the agenda, minutes, handouts, and other important information in a safe and predetermined place after the meeting. There should be a system in place to file these documents so they can be found in the future.

These are things that need to be done to end the actual meeting and to wrap up all meeting-related tasks. It is good to have a standard procedure to handle these duties in a timely and organized manner. Following through on all of these things will help your attendees, co-workers, supervisors, and others to realize that you take the meetings seriously and want to handle them in the right way.

CONCLUSION

I n the introduction I asked what you think of when someone mentions
meetings. I hope that you have a different picture in your mind after
reading this book. Meetings can be a painful and frustrating experience,
but by implementing the information in this book you can hold productive
and effective meetings.

Preparation determines meeting success. I am talking about preparation by
everyone who will be at the meeting. Obviously the leader and facilitator
need to prepare for the meeting. The agenda needs to be organized in
a thorough way to ensure the important topics are discussed. After the
agenda is finished, it needs to be distributed to the attendees to allow time
for them to prepare for the meeting. Preparation is a key element of an
effective meeting.

We discussed different types of meetings and how to evaluate whether you
need a meeting. If there is another effective way to resolve the situation,
it should be used. We had a chapter on how to choose the right location
for your meeting, when to schedule it, and whom to invite. Each of these
decision will affect the success of your meeting.

The correct location and setup will make a difference in the effectiveness of
your meeting. The setup should be based on what you need to accomplish

and the number of people who will attend. It is good to evaluate the setup and room to be used for each meeting individually.

Meeting tools and equipment can affect your meeting. When you do not have the tools and equipment you need, the meeting is directly affected. This is also true when you decide who will speak in your meeting.

Each of these subjects may not seem very important to some people, but combine all the elements that were discussed and you have the recipe for a successful and effective meeting. As a final note, remember that the suggestions and information in this book are guidelines for you to use when creating and planning the most effective meetings possible. The actual strategies you should use will be determined by your leadership style and the individual needs of your attendees. Best wishes on holding the most effective meetings possible in your future.

APPENDIX:
TERM MEANINGS

A

Acceptance – Signing a contract.

Acknowledgement – Written notice of confirmation for a guest.

Actual Budget – Current, real budget.

Advance Deposit – The money paid in advance to secure a room or refreshments.

Advance Registration – Allowing potential attendees to register before the event.

Agenda – An outline, list, or plan to be followed for the meeting.

Arbitration – A procedure used to resolve problems or dispute without going to court.

Attendee Data – Demographic information about each attendee.

Audio Conferencing – A live meeting on the phone.

Authorized Signature – The signature of person who can make and approve decisions.

Auxiliary Business – An outside business that is involved in a meeting.

Auxiliary Service – Outside services which are needed for the meeting.

B

Badge – A tag which is used to identify attendees.

Banquet – A fancy meal served to a number of people and can be to recognize someone.

Banquet Event Order – A form which is used to list all the details about a banquet.

Board of Directors Style – Double width table used for conferences.

Book – To schedule an event in advance.

Breakout Sessions – When meeting participants are divided into small groups to work together on specific tasks for the group.

Business Casual – A less formal style of dress instead of a suit and tie or dress.

C

Cancellation Clause – A contract clause which outlines the damages if the contract is terminated.

Cash Bar – Bar service at an event where the attendees pay cash for alcoholic drinks.

Classroom Style – When seats are arranged in rows and face the conductor. All attendees have a place to take notes.

Clause – A portion of a contract which pertains to a specific subject.

Complete Meeting Package – A plan which includes all meals, lodging, and services.

Complimentary Room – A meeting room which is furnished at no charge.

Conference Style – When seats are arranged around all sides of the tables.

Confirmation – When reservations are verified.

Confirmation Letter – A written verification of a reservation.

Conflict of Interest – A document that requires a speaker to reveal any conflicts with your organization.

Contract – A legally binding agreement between parties.

D

Demographic Profile – Group statistical information about participants, including age, location, gender, income, and other details.

Double Booked – When more than one group is booked for the same location at the same time.

Dress Code – A type and style of clothing that is acceptable.

Duty Roster – An hourly schedule which outlines all of the staff member duties.

F

Facilitator – A person expected to keep the meeting on track and effective.

Floor Plan – A drawing to scale which shows the room arrangement.

Function – A planned meeting.

Function Sheet – The details relating to a planned meeting.

Function Space – An area which is reserved for a meeting.

G

Gratuity – A percentage of the bill which is paid to the staff for a meeting.

H

Head Count – The number of people in attendance.

Host – A person who will assist speaker before, during, and after meeting.

I

Incidentals – Minor expenses which are not detailed.

Invitation Letter – A letter sent to a potential speaker asking them to attend your meeting.

K

Keynote – The opening statement or remarks.

Keynote Speaker – A person who gives the primary speech.

L

Lectern – A stand which is elevated to hold reading materials, notes, or visual aids.

M

Meeting History – Information and details about past meetings.

Meeting Profile – A report with details about former meetings.

Moderator – A person who oversees the meeting.

N

Networking – A chance to exchange information between people and businesses.

No-Show Report – A report that details the attendees who do not show up and did not cancel.

O

Off-Site Event – Meetings held somewhere other than your office or business.

Outside Vendor – A vendor who provides services for a meeting or event.

Outsourcing – Bringing in people from the outside to work on a meeting or event.

Overbooking – Scheduling multiple events or meetings on a specific day, time, and location.

P

Program Development – Planning before an event to determine content and format.

R

Reasonable Accommodation – Facilities must make reasonable efforts to accommodate people with disabilities or hardships.

Registrant – A meeting attendee who is registered beforehand.

Report – The details used to evaluate meeting.

Room Capacity – The total number of people who can be in a room comfortably.

S

Skirting – The fabric placed around the bottom of tables for a meeting or event.

Staging Guide – A notebook that contains room layouts, function sheets, and any other information needed for meetings or events.

T

Table Top Display – Visual aids that are placed on top of a table.

Teleconferencing – People from different regions meeting without leaving their locations. The live feed enables the participants to interact with each other.

V

Video Conference – Video monitors that are set up and connected through phone lines, satellite, or ground wires allowing people to meet "face-to-face" with no regard to their physical location. The conference can include visual clips, graphics, and data or document transmissions.

W

Webcasting – When words, pictures, audio, and visual elements are delivered over the Internet.

BUSINESS MEETING – RESOURCE LIST

101 Ways to Make Meetings Active: Surefire Ideas to Engage Your Group, by Mel Silberman, Kathy Clark, Pfeiffer.

Effective Meeting Skills A Practical Guide for More Productive Meetings How to Plan and Conduct High Quality Meetings, by Marion E. Haynes, Crisp Publications, Inc., Menlo Park, California.

Fat Free Meetings How to Make Them Fast, Focused and Fun!, by Burt Albert, Peterson's, Princeton, New Jersey.

First Aid for Meetings: Quick Fixes and Major Repairs for Running Effective Meetings, by Charlie Hawkins, Bookpartners.

Great Meetings! Great Results, by Dee Kelsey, Pam Plumb, Beth Braganca, Hanson Park Press, Inc., Rev & Expand edition.

How to Hold Successful Meetings: 30 Action Tips for Managing Effective Meetings (30-Minute Solutions Series), by Paul R. Timm, Career Press.

How to Make Meetings Work, by Michael Doyle, Jove.

Last Minute Meetings, by Fern Dickey, CMP, Career Press, Franklin Lakes, New Jersey.

Meetings, Meetings and More Meetings: Getting Things Done When People Are Involved, by Simon Ramo Ph.D., Bonus Books, Santa Monica, California.

Running a Meeting That Works (Barron's Business Success Series), by Robert F. Miller, Marilyn Pincus, Barron's Educational Series; 3rd Edition.

The Manager's Guide to Effective Meetings, by Barbara J. Streibel, McGraw-Hill.

Tools for Facilitating Meetings Easy Ways to Help Plan, Organize, Conduct and Evaluate Team Meetings, by Johnna L. Howell, Integrity Publishing, Seattle, Washington.

365 Foolish Mistakes Smart Managers Commit Every Day: How and Why to Avoid Them - by Shri Henkel, Atlantic Publishing, Ocala, Florida.

AUTHOR BIOGRAPHY

S hri Henkel lives in the Shenandoah Valley of Virginia. Her desire to write began at an early age. She has finally been able to reach the goal of seeing her books in print, under her given name and her pen name. Shri owns a Management and Marketing Consulting business and is a freelance writer and marketing professional.

This is one of her four non-fiction books being released in 2006-2007. Each focuses on business management. One is a guide for first-time managers. One book is specifically targeted to pizza and sub shop managers or owners, while the third focuses on non-commercial food service management. Each will be available from Atlantic Publishing.

Shri has 21 years of business management and 16 years of marketing experience. The knowledge she gained in this work has been invaluable in creating helpful handbooks for business managers and owners. These experiences include suggestions about techniques that worked and warnings about things that didn't.

In addition to her non fiction work, she has four novels in print under her pen name, Nikki Leigh. She is beginning work on her fifth and sixth novels and two novellas. Her love of the coast, history, and lighthouses is apparent in her stories. On a trip to Cape Ann with her brother, Chris, she discovered the area that was the perfect setting for a series of books. The rugged land, hard working people, and rich history were too compelling to ignore. Cape Ann, Eastern Point, and Gloucester, Massachusetts are the setting for her books which focus on the "Stormy View" lighthouse. Her first novella is set along the Outer Banks of North Carolina and is the first mystery in a series.

For more information about her work, visit her fiction Web site at **www.nikkileigh.com** or her business site **www.sandcconsulting.com**. She also invites you to visit her and other friends at the Readers Station. This site helps readers understand more about the settings and characters that make up your favorite stories. You also have a chance to meet and talk with authors. The Web site is: **www.readersstation.com**.

INDEX

KEEP YOUR BUSINESS RUNNING SMOOTHLY

HOW TO HIRE, TRAIN & KEEP THE BEST EMPLOYEES FOR YOUR SMALL BUSINESS: WITH COMPANION CD-ROM

Getting the right people in the right job and then getting them to stay are the key elements in effective business organizations. It sounds straightforward, and many people simply put an ad in the paper, wait for the applications, do some interviewing, and then hire the people they liked the best. Boom, done! Then all hell starts breaking loose: there are attendance problems, attitude problems, and personality conflicts; the business is suffering; the employees are suffering; and management is barely able to keep the ship afloat. What went wrong? The short answer is they hired the wrong people; they failed to make human resource management a priority. The good news is that careful planning and strategic management of the recruitment, hiring and retention processes will greatly improve success; the bad news is that HR management is not an exact science because people are unpredictable. Fortunately, there are many strategies, techniques and practices proven to improve all aspects of people management. These are the skills you'll learn in *How to Hire, Train & Keep the Best Employees for Your Small Business.* **288 Pages • Item # HTK-02 • $29.95**

365 WAY TO MOTIVATE AND REWARD YOUR EMPLOYEES EVERY DAY—WITH LITTLE OR NO MONEY

This book is packed with hundreds of simple and inexpensive ways to motivate, challenge and reward your employees. Employees need constant re-enforcement and recognition—and here's how to do it. You will find real-life, proven examples and case studies from actual companies that you can put to use immediately. You can use this book daily to boost morale, productivity and profits. This is your opportunity to build an organization that people love to work at with these quick, effective, humorous, innovative and simply fun solutions to challenges. **288 Pages • Item # 365-01 • $24.95**

501+ GREAT INTERVIEW QUESTIONS FOR EMPLOYERS AND THE BEST ANSWERS FOR PROSPECTIVE EMPLOYEES

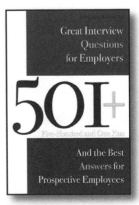

For anyone who hires employees, this is a must-have book. It is also essential for anyone searching for a new job or going on a job interview. Once you learn the right questions to ask, you'll get the best employees. As you know, it is not always the best candidate that gets the job—but often the person who interviews the best. For the prospective employee, learn how to sell yourself and get the job you want! **288 Pages • Item # 501-02 • $24.95**

To order call 1-800-814-1132 or visit www.atlantic-pub.com

GETTING CLIENTS AND KEEPING CLIENTS FOR YOUR SERVICE BUSINESS: A 30-DAY STEP-BY-STEP PLAN FOR BUILDING YOUR BUSINESS

This is the only book written for the small business service provider. In 30 days or less, you will be so successful attracting business that you can select clients you want to serve. This specialized book will demonstrate how to market and promote your services easily, inexpensively, and profitably. You will learn how to find new clients quickly and keep existing ones satisfied by selling client-based solutions and services. Put technology and low-cost marketing devices into place with little or no time. Learn to develop a marketing plan with hundreds of practical ideas to attract new clients and increase business with existing ones.

288 Pgs • Item #GCK-01 • $24.95

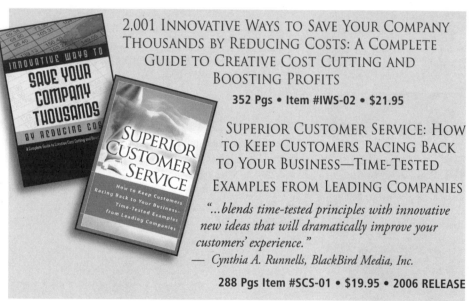

2,001 INNOVATIVE WAYS TO SAVE YOUR COMPANY THOUSANDS BY REDUCING COSTS: A COMPLETE GUIDE TO CREATIVE COST CUTTING AND BOOSTING PROFITS

352 Pgs • Item #IWS-02 • $21.95

SUPERIOR CUSTOMER SERVICE: HOW TO KEEP CUSTOMERS RACING BACK TO YOUR BUSINESS—TIME-TESTED EXAMPLES FROM LEADING COMPANIES

"...blends time-tested principles with innovative new ideas that will dramatically improve your customers' experience."
— Cynthia A. Runnells, BlackBird Media, Inc.

288 Pgs Item #SCS-01 • $19.95 • 2006 RELEASE

365 ANSWERS ABOUT HUMAN RESOURCES FOR THE SMALL BUSINESS OWNER: WHAT EVERY MANAGER NEEDS TO KNOW ABOUT WORKPLACE LAW

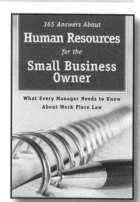

Finally there is a complete and up-to-date resource for the small business owner. Tired of high legal and consulting fees? This new book is your answer! Detailed are over 300 common questions employers have about employees and the law; it's like having an employment attorney on your staff.

288 Pages • Item # HRM-02 • $21.95